P9-APE-017

BLACK WOMEN
INC.

25 Stories That Gave Birth to a Company

Annette Y. Britton

© 2009

5 Black Women, Inc.

By Annette Y. Britton

© 2009 Annette Y. Britton. All rights reserved.

No part of this publication may be reproduced or transmitted in any form
or by any means, mechanical or electronic, including photocopying and
recording, or by any information storage and retrieval system, without
permission in writing from author or publisher (except by a reviewer, who
may quote brief passages and/or show brief video clips in a review).

ISBN: 978-0-9822206-6-5
Library of Congress Control Number: 2009938859

www.fiveblackwomen.com

Published by Writers of the Round Table Press
Cover Design by Nathan Brown
Edited by Eva Silva Travers and Corey Blake
Layout by Sunny B. DiMartino

I dedicate this to my son and my mama.

The names and identifying details of some individuals mentioned in this book have been changed.

INTRODUCTION

The course of my life has never been a straight line; instead, it has dipped and curved, filled with experiences that crash against each other and pull away—experiences that share few similarities on the surface. For example, there's the time in 1970 when carloads of Mennonites helped build our inner city Chicago home. Then there was the time when I was a child that my mama breathed life into a frozen puppy before our awe-filled eyes, and, of course, the day my brother won the lottery and changed our family's life forever. But when I look deeply, I realize that the stories of my life have one thing in common; always, they have asked me to think deeply about who I am and what I want to offer the world.

On June 22, 2007, I found myself in The Dreaming Room. The brainchild of small business guru Michael Gerber, The Dreaming Room challenged us participants to **think big** and to share our stories. To my surprise, my own poured out of me, finally busting open the traffic jam they had caused in my mind. For the first time in years, my stories weren't stuck. They had momentum. That meant that new ideas could finally push through as well.

This book—a collection of the most meaningful, miraculous, and bizarre experiences of my life—is the birth of a business I've had in my mind for years. It's called Five Black Women, Inc., and the concept was born nearly two decades ago. I was an electronic engineer at Xerox at the time, and I thought, *why can't there be a corporation started by black women like me?* The white men around me were no smarter than I was, after all. I thought, *five black women. That's a force that can make something happen.*

Today, I want Five Black Women, Inc. to help redefine what we think of as "community." We need to create communities in the truest sense of the word—by enabling people to connect with one another based on common interest, not just location. I want Five Black Women, Inc. to pull people together based on problems they want to solve, like fighting crime in their neighborhood or ensuring that their kids can go to college. The company will take some of the best corporate training I've had and use it to equip people with skills they need to solve their problems. It's time to make a difference in this world, and we *can*—by empowering people at the community level.

The world is not created or sustained by superstars; it's the everyday, average people like you and me who can truly make an impact. In reading this book, I hope you'll see that everybody has something to offer. Everybody has a story worth telling. And I hope you'll ask yourself—as I have throughout my life—*What is my purpose here?* When you discover that purpose, allow it to stir and break free within you. Fly with it and offer the world a greater good. Be the person that the voice inside of you wants you to become.

The Stories

Dad Gets Shot

Up to a point, all of my earliest childhood recollections are kind of hazy and unclear, just sketchy images here and there. One, though, is as clear and vivid as a Technicolor memory in motion. It has never dimmed, and I don't expect it ever will. It's the night that my dad got shot.

I must have been three or four years old. I was a late talker and a shy, clingy child, always shadowing my mama everywhere she went. Because I was tongue-tied, I guess I took comfort in knowing that my mother understood me—or at least tried to—even when no one else did. She and my grandmother used to spend time with me on their laps, teaching me how to say very simple words. The bottom line was that it seemed I almost always had a handful of Mama's skirt. In almost every early picture of me, I wasn't looking at the camera; I was looking up at my mother.

I don't remember if I actually heard the phone ring, but somehow I knew that Mama was up in the middle of the night. Standing behind her, I heard her start to cry, and a feeling that something terrible had happened filled my body. By the time she hung up the phone, I knew that my father had been shot and that my mother had to go to the hospital to be with him. I didn't know what those two things meant for me and I didn't know how to express how scared I was.

Dad was a stationary engineer working in the boiler room at American Hospital in Chicago. Well, for some reason, he had either gone to the back door or had been outside in the back of the building. The details are hazy, but two guys were out there, demanding to be let in that back door. One had been shot a couple of times. My dad was a stubborn cuss, and there was seldom talking him into anything under any circumstances. He didn't know what was going on, was not about to allow either man in that way, and told them to go around to the emergency entrance like everyone else. As Dad would later tell the story to me over and over again, he turned to go back inside, and

1

the next thing he knew, he simultaneously heard a single gunshot and felt a searing pain in his back. He'd been hit by a single shot to the spine… by an off-duty police officer.

Dad's legs were instantly paralyzed. He was probably fifty-four then, and Mama would have been twenty-seven. Everything changed that day. I don't know how long it actually was, but it felt like a year before I saw my father again. And all of a sudden, Mama had to go to work to help support the family while all of the litigation was going on. Believe it or not, we kids only got to see him one time during his hospital stay. I remember standing there, holding on to Mama and seeing my daddy in a wheelchair. It was the first time I'd seen him in months, and he gave us all big hugs. I'm sure we would have seen more of him, but Mama was trying to work and take care of my brother, sisters, and me all on her own. Life was hard for her then, no doubt about it.

The whole incident was mysterious. The other guy who'd been shot recovered completely, but considering that the shooter was an off-duty officer, the single newspaper article about the incident was awfully tiny. Of course, Dad sued the Chicago Police Department, but in retrospect, everything seemed hush-hush; all settlements happened outside of the court.

Dad kept the settlement a mystery, too. As Mama tells it, he called her to the hospital one time. A lawyer was there, and Dad—whom Mama called Archie—had a paper that said she wouldn't sue the guy who'd shot him, or something like that. Now, I don't know exactly how much the offer was, but I know that Mama was upset about it, and Daddy just kept saying, "It's okay; just sign it!" So, she did, and the lawyer plopped the check in her hand. And that was that.

You can bet there was a larger settlement, but Mama and we kids never saw a dime of it. Here's where things get complicated. Some time after that initial "settlement," Mama went to the hospital to visit only to be told that Daddy had been discharged. He was nowhere in sight. Come to find out, he'd taken his settlement money and moved in with his mother and his sister Ernestine in the back of her beauty salon. He had no intention of coming home.

Well, you know what they say about a woman scorned. Mama gathered all of us around her at the kitchen table and asked us point blank if we wanted our daddy. We said, yes, of course we did! She told the five of us, "He's over at your aunt's house, but we're gonna get your father!" When Mama made up her mind about something, there was no changing it. She hatched a plan and made sure that we were all a part of it. When we descended on the apartment behind the salon, we'd wait for the signal from Mama, the nod of her head. With that, one of us was supposed to grab Daddy's crutches, one was supposed to grab his bag of clothes, and so on.

So, we went over to Aunt Ernestine's under the guise of a nice visit. After she let us in and went back to her salon, Mama talked with Daddy for a few minutes. She mentioned coming home, but before it had a chance to turn ugly, we got the signal and sprung into action. I'll never forget the sight of my mother leaning over the bed and scooping up my father. He started screaming to high heaven, and Ernestine tried to come to the rescue. Well, Mama was nothing if not prepared; she pulled a small billy club out of her bosom and started waving it around. Ernestine flipped and was running around yelling, "She's got a gun! She's got a gun!" The last thing we saw of her was her backside as she ran out.

Somehow, Mama managed to carry Daddy all the way out to the car. It was quite a sight with him carrying on like a madman and her saying, quite simply, "No, you're coming home with your family." She put him in the car, we drove home, and the issue was settled.

Daddy never stopped talking about the money he'd supposedly left under the pillow. Ernestine certainly never brought it to him, and his own mother sent a letter with some pittance in it telling him it was all the money he'd ever need. He also never stopped cursing; he started a tirade the moment Mama scooped him up and never stopped until the day he died.

5

DONNA SAVES ANNETTE

Mama always had a gift, a way of knowing things and seeing things. They weren't dreams or feelings. She called them premonitions, and that's exactly what they were. She shared them with us; they became just part and parcel of our daily lives. She knew she was in God's hands, which meant that her children were, too, so her premonitions were evidence of His guidance and reassurance.

I don't remember when I heard it the first time. I just grew up understanding that my mother knew that she would lose one of us, that either one of my sisters or my brother or I would not grow up to be an adult. What a burden for a mother to carry, to know one of her babies would not live very long. I don't remember thinking about it much, maybe because adulthood seemed so far away. It felt like I would live forever even before I got that far. Anyway, Mama said that God spoke to her… and that's one of the things he told her.

That knowledge must have kind of hung over Mama, because even then it seemed to me like she was looking for signs to try to figure out who it was going to be, which one of her babies would leave. For a while, she thought it was me. What none of us could have known, though, is that one of her other babies would actually save my life.

I was about seven or eight years old, so it was 1965. A bunch of kids in the neighborhood were going to Mrs. Stevens' Bible class. It was new and gave us something different from the usual to do. I went with the rest of the little kids, my sisters included. I don't remember if my brother went or not; he was much older. I can still hear the words of that old song: "Come to Bible class, come to Bible class, every Friday afternoon come to Bible class." And every Friday afternoon, that's what we did. We would all sit around together and listen to the Bible stories, as told by the Moody Bible Institute students, and I loved it! The tales just came to life there on the storyboard with all of the little felt figures and scenes being moved around by the hands of Moody students who told the stories with so much love and conviction. I remember how seeing the excitement on the other faces made my excitement all the sweeter. One day, I gave my soul to Jesus right then and there in that Bible class. I guessed I'd had plenty of chances to get saved at church, but I made the connection there with my little friends. I was thrilled and ran home to tell Mama all about it. I couldn't wait to share the good news.

Well, Mama cried, but not tears of joy. She was so distraught, and I didn't understand.

She told me later that since God had saved me that way, I must be the one he was going to take home. I didn't know what to think.

Around that same time, I spent a lot of my afternoons at the library with my oldest sister, Donna, whenever mama would let us. Donna was so smart; she eventually became Valedictorian of her 8th grade class. I loved doing most anything with her. When we moved to the new house, the two of us were going to share a room, while my other two sisters would share another. "Roommates!" I said. I don't think Donna was as excited about sharing a room with her little sister as I was to be sharing a room with her.

One particular time, we were walking down the street to the library— kind of a busy street—and this guy jumped out of an alley and grabbed me! He had my arm and wouldn't let go. I squirmed and pulled with all my might but couldn't budge as he tried and tried to pull me into the alley. Well, he never even got me off of the sidewalk! Donna had me by the other arm, and she was even more determined than he was not to let go. I'm sure it lasted less than thirty seconds, but I felt like I was in the middle of a never-ending tug of war. I was so little, but the memories are so clear. I saw little thought bubbles, like the ones in the cartoons, before me somehow. In those bubbles were images of my father, my mother, my whole family, and they were fading in and out one after the other. I had a sickening feeling that I would never see them again.

All of a sudden an ear-piercing, "Let go of my sister!" shook me back to reality and burst the last bubble. With a final yank and tug, I flew into my sister, and the guy went running down the alley. Terror and trauma shot through me as my knees knocked together. They felt wobbly, like jello. I must have been in a hysterical daze or something, because next thing I knew, Donna smacked me right across the face to get me under control. The first words out of her mouth were, "Don't you ever tell Mama this happened or she will never let us go to the library again!" I don't remember if we went on to the library, although I'm pretty sure we did, or went on home; it didn't matter to me. I was just happy to be alive.

The next thing I knew, Donna got sick. A year or two later, Mama lost her baby, just like God had told her. I kept our secret, Donna's and mine, until I was probably thirty years old or so. It spilled right out of me during a holiday gathering, as we prepared dinner in the kitchen. Mama shook her head with a little smile, and we all thought about Donna, a guardian angel even before she left us.

Tippy!

My mama is an exceptional woman. Always has been. She's just always had a way of knowing things, of understanding if they were meant to be and how they were supposed to happen. When she's got something in her mind, there is no way around it. Well, that was a lucky thing for our dog Tippy.

Tippy's mother was our dog Lassie. We were all little kids the winter that Lassie was full of puppies. She was a good dog, well-trained, thanks to Mama. We didn't care anything about specific breeds; to us she was just a dog with a pretty red coat. We called her a bird dog because our neighbor took her bird hunting every year. There in the house with us, she was safe from the bitter cold—and was a constant reminder to us that there'd soon be more dogs to love. We couldn't wait.

Well, out of the clear blue one day, my dad decided that the dog did not belong in the house—especially when she was birthing pups— and told us to put her outside. God only knows how cold it was outside, and there was no doghouse! Mama argued back and forth with him for a while, and somehow Dad conceded that we could put her under the house. It was an old house with space underneath for storing coal. The entrance was on the side of the house, and was big enough for bringing in and shoveling the coal. So that's where Lassie went.

Blankets and all, we got her settled down there, knowing that she would have those pups any day. We all took turns checking on her and making sure she was as warm as could be. I remember her lying there moaning, going through early labor, I guess. I was so little then; I just wanted the pups to arrive! We'd cover her up, spend a few minutes rubbing her, but then get too cold and run back on inside.

Finally, several of us went outside to check on her and, sure enough, she was giving birth. There were a few puppies close to her… but one pushed off to the side. He was stiff! Oh my God, we were all so scared. We grabbed that puppy and ran in the house. "Mama,

7

we've got a frozen puppy!" we all yelled, clamoring around her.

Well, that was it. "Go out there right now and bring in Lassie and those pups! I don't care what your dad says!" We handed off the little black puppy to Mama and set off on our mission. I don't know whether she somehow *knew* that that puppy was so supposed to live or whether she *decided* it was supposed to live, but she was rubbing it between her hands before we reached the door. When we came back in with Lassie and the others, she was standing over the gas space heater, an old fashioned thing with a flue and flame at the top. That puppy was getting warmed at a distance by the flame and by Mama's insistent hands. All of us huddled around with anxious faces as she rubbed and rubbed some more. We all looked at each other and back at Mama when she gave the lifeless body mouth-to-mouth. Rubbing, warming, breathing… again and again.

Suddenly, he moved! Just a little bit, but he moved. Mama kept up the routine. He twitched again and then again. It was such an awesome sight to see my mother bring this puppy back to life. And he was…he was alive, thanks to her. I remember watching her feed it with an eyedropper, after we warmed the milk on the stove as she told us to do. Then we all begged for the chance to hold and feed this little "living miracle." There were quite a few pups in that litter, but Tippy was the one that got to stay. There was no putting any of them back outside, and Daddy never said a word about it.

From day one, Tippy was a very smart dog. Probably because we'd seen him come to life, he was more like another sibling than a pet to us. He grew to be a pretty good-sized dog, looking something like a black Labrador but with a thicker coat, like a German shepherd. He loved to sit and watch TV with us. He'd let us ride on his back. And he never once snapped at us or bit us. He sure loved Mama, and spent a lot of time hanging out with her in the kitchen.

I really don't know how old Tippy was, but he was full grown when the time came to move into the house that Dad was building for us. It was right around the fall of 1969, and Lassie was pregnant again. Dad lowered the boom again and announced that there would be NO animals coming to the new house; we were supposed to simply leave them behind.

We moved over the course of a week or so, filling and refilling a little trailer that hooked to the back of the car. We filled the trailer with the very last load, and the plan was all in place. Mom left a whole bag of dog food for Tippy and Lassie, and when we got to the new house she would call the pound or whatever and have the dogs picked up. We said our goodbyes to Lassie, but when we called for Tippy, he was nowhere to be found. Sadly, we piled in the car while Dad fussed and fumed for us to hurry up.

With a last look back as we pulled down the street, my brother and sisters and I saw something that made us cheer. There was Tippy, running behind us! "Stop the car! Stop the car!" we yelled, and Daddy yelled right back that there would be NO dogs at the new house and told Mama to keep driving. We made our way slowly down the alley but picked up speed on the main street; Tippy knew something was up and was running for dear life. He was running so hard and keeping up as we turned onto Talman Ave., with us kids cheering him on. Finally, we had to turn on to Washington Boulevard, a four-lane, one-way street, and Mama had no choice but to pick up speed. Dad must've been pretty sure of himself because he said, "If that dog makes it to the new house, we'll keep him."

It was a Sunday, as I recall, and there wasn't a lot of traffic. At first, Tippy stayed right behind us. Then the cars got too close, and he moved to the sidewalk. With more traffic and more speed, he was slowly falling behind. He made it through one intersection first and then two more but was farther behind each time. With just one more traffic light to go before reaching the new house, we lost sight of our Tippy. By then, we were all concerned that he may have gotten hit. All of us sad and quiet, we pulled into the alley behind our new home.

We had to get Daddy in first. Once he was settled, Mama circled the block to go back and see if we could spot Tippy. We found no sign of him, nothing. We were happy to see he hadn't been hurt on the street but sad that we lost track of him. Once again, we pulled into the alley, this time to unload the trailer. As we opened the back gate, there before our startled eyes were red paw prints going up the walkway to the side door of the house. We ran in, and there was Tippy, lying on the floor, nursing a bad cut on his paw. Mama wrapped his paw in a towel, and she and my brother set off to find a vet to sew it up. He was a little worse for wear, but he had found our new home!

It had taken four years to build that new house. During those years, our car had made a lot of trips back and forth from the old house. I think that somehow, whether it was his sense of smell or not, Tippy was just tuned in to the general direction the car went and then to the scent of his family. I guess we'll never know for sure, but he'd fought hard to be with us in the first place, and he didn't give up easily.

And so he stayed with us. Everybody loved Tippy, and he seemed to know it. He sort of became the neighborhood dog. We never actually saw him leap the chain link fence around the yard—coming or going—but he got out all the time, and almost everyone in the neighborhood had stories of Tippy's adventures. He loved to hang out at Al's Hot Dogs, which was about four blocks away. People would see him there and say, "Tippy, go home!" He'd hang his head, all dejected, like he was just trying to hang out with the other dogs and get some good eats, and finally walk away

Tippy found his way into plenty of trouble, too. He got out of the yard a lot at night. Sometimes he came home smelling terrible. One time, he came home looking like he was all wet. When I pulled my hand away from his black fur, though, it was covered in blood. He'd been in a terrible dogfight and had bites and scratches all over him. Fortunately, my brother was a teenager by then and worked part-time at a hospital. I guess he'd been taking notes, because he doctored Tippy right up! He laid out a white sheet on the table and washed and sutured Tippy's wounds himself. Good thing, because we certainly couldn't afford to take him to the vet all the time.

Tippy was a leader, too. When my grandma moved into the building, she brought her Cocker Spaniel with her. His name was Quien Es? which means, "*Who is it?*" in Spanish. Tippy was the leader of the pack, the head honcho. That Spaniel and every other dog that ever lived at our house ended up following Tippy around, even on his nighttime prowls out of the yard. In the morning, my mom would call and call Tippy before finally giving up and slamming the door. A few minutes later, there he'd be, and he knew he was in for a scolding. Whenever he would come home without Quien Es, Mama would yell, "Where's Quien Es? Don't you come home without him! You go get him and bring him home." I swear, a few minutes later, there they'd both be on the porch! Tippy always took the scolding, because he always knew that Mama would end up letting him in the house.

Well, he got even smarter. One time, after a particularly good scolding, he hobbled in with a hurt paw. Mama got all soft and babied him, of course. He was no fool. Every time after that when he knew he was in trouble, he would start limping for sympathy! We kids knew what he was up to, and we'd always distract him, get him excited to play. He'd end up running around, and we'd say, "Ah! You're busted!" He'd stop and hang his head, and Mama would laugh.

I guess with all of his trips about town, Tippy developed mange. Year after year it got worse, the red irritated spot with hair loss. The vet told my mom what to do for it, but every summer it just seemed to get worse. Finally, it seemed to engulf practically the whole rear quarter of his body, and he would just moan miserably. Mama had always talked to him, and I swear he understood. One time as she was petting him she said, "I may have to put you to sleep." Before that season ended, Tippy just went away. We searched out all of his haunts and asked everyone if they'd seen him. We never found hide or hair of our Tippy. We were all sad, especially Mama.

Tippy lived with us for probably eight or so years. Like Mama, he had a way of knowing things, especially the fact that he belonged with us. I'm glad that the two of them agreed on that fact that day over the space heater when Mama brought warmth and breath into his little body.

DONNA LEAVES US

I got to have my sister Donna for just a couple more years after she saved my own life. It all happened so fast; we were so young. Again, Donna was so smart. She graduated from the 8th grade as Valedictorian of her class. We went through the summer, having a great time, doing all of those things that kids do: swimming, playing, spending long days. Little did we know that it would be our last summer together.

It was September 1967. Donna had just started high school. Just about a week into it, she started complaining about pain in her sides and her stomach. Of course, at first, Mama thought it was just a normal childhood illness, something that would pass. It just kept getting worse, though, and fast. Finally, Donna missed a couple days of school. That's probably when we all knew that it was something serious; that girl loved school and would never *choose* to miss a day.

Mama decided she'd better take Donna to the hospital. Afterward, Mama came home without my sister, telling all of us that they were going to do exploratory surgery on her because they didn't know what was wrong. I remember Daddy getting really angry, yelling at my mother for telling all of us kids what was going on. I also remember crying and crying because I was so scared; I just didn't understand what was happening to my sister. I was nine, and she was fourteen. I never saw Donna again.

It turned out that Donna had a tumor. It was something called Wilms' tumor, and it engulfed her entire kidney. The exploratory surgery found it inoperable, so the doctors tried radiation. She was just so sick, and all of us kids were really too young to be carted back and forth to the hospital. Besides, back in those days kids weren't even allowed in the hospital rooms. Exactly three weeks to the day that my sister entered the hospital, she died there. It was October 4, 1967.

Looking back on those three weeks, it all seemed sort of unreal. I mean, I guess at times like those, life has to go on to a certain extent. Mama had to go to work. We all had to go to school. I remember, too, seeing my brother practice his karate. One time, he had hit Donna across the back with a broomstick while doing his moves. For the longest time, I thought that that blow caused her sickness. Of course, that wasn't the case, but it made sense to me as a kid. I was just looking for answers.

I'll never forget the day Donna died. We kids always came home for lunch. For some reason I was really excited about these papers I brought home to be signed; they were probably for a field trip or something like that. Well, I ran in the door, and everyone was there: My brother was sitting on the sofa, red-faced and crying, and my mother was in the back room, crying, too, of course. My aunt took me aside and told me that my sister had died. I guess I just didn't—maybe couldn't—let it sink in then. I kept insisting on my papers being signed. "I have to take this back to school!" I said. My aunt signed it. I don't remember eating lunch, but I'm sure I did, and then I rushed back to school.

It didn't hit me until later. I guess my family must have called the school, because my teacher pulled me out of class to talk to me. Her name was Mrs. McGuff, and she had been Donna's teacher at one time, too. Anyway, there we were, just the two of us. She told me how happy she was that I'd brought back the forms… and then she told me how sorry she was about Donna and how important it was that I go home. I started crying and couldn't stop. Somebody—I don't remember who—came to get me, and I went straight home to be with my family.

We had kind of a big extended family, so by the time I was nine years old, I'd been to a number of funerals: Bubba, my grandmother on my Dad's side, and Granny, my great-grandmother, for instance. The first funeral I cried at, though, was my sister's. I remember going to the little local funeral home and then on to the repast at Aunt Beulah's house. There was always lots of food at these kinds of gatherings, potluck style, with everyone contributing. Even before the funeral itself, people were so kind and generous, bringing food for days on

end, which was good because Mama was just kind of in a daze, not able to function very well.

Usually families gather at home after funerals. However, we were so poor that our house was in no condition for a lot of visitors. Fortunately, there was Aunt Beulah's house, which was always the place for family gatherings, and that was the important thing. The extended family reached out to help us. All of the cousins were there, but I was still so shy at that time. Donna had always been the social one. I remember thinking that if she had been there—if this had been someone else's funeral—she would've been running around with all the other kids while I was glued to Mama's leg. But me, I was simply hanging onto my Mama.

Sears Roebuck
and the Swimming Pool

Like most kids, one of our favorite things to do—my sisters, my brother, and I—was go to the beach on our summer breaks, or any time for that matter. Mama was always so good about taking us. We'd pack up a lunch and off we'd go for the day. It was great to get out of the neighborhood and just spend the day having fun.

Well, every once in a while, there was some strange thing that happened, something that seems even stranger now than it did then. For some reason, sometimes the water at the Twelfth Street Beach would just be brimming with dead fish. They'd be bobbing and floating all over the place, but usually pretty far out. As a young kid, you don't really stop to wonder just what is actually *causing* the fish to die; you just know that you came to swim and as long as the fish are past your fun-zone, all is well.

This one particular day, things were different. The fish were actually washing up on the shore, completely intruding on our swimming area. The smell was horrendous, but we all insisted on going in anyway. We managed to dodge most of the fish and have a little fun before Mama just couldn't stand any more and came to drag us out. We probably weren't there for fifteen minutes before we trekked back across the sand. To this day, I have no idea why the fish died there, how frequently the mass deaths occurred, or why it was so bad on that particular day. For me at the time, it was just more of an inconvenience and a disappointment.

For Mama, it was the cause for a resolution. She did NOT want us in that water. Then and there she decided that we would have a swimming pool. Now, for us inner-city kids, the idea of a swimming pool was just plain bizarre. It makes me laugh to look back on that day because Mama always asked me—the whole time I was growing up—where I got my big ideas from. I think I know exactly where I got them from!

We had moved from the old neighborhood into the new house by then and I guess the pool was just another part of the overall change in lifestyle, even though we were still in the heart of the city.

We didn't get the pool that summer, but Mama must have saved money over the course of the next year, because the following summer found us with a pool. I was in the sixth grade, and one day Mama and the four of us kids set off to the Sears Roebuck store. There in the pool department, we were just thrilled. There were so many options. There were also two different salesmen. One was white, and one was black.

Mama went right over to the black sales guy, an older, mature man. She started talking to him about what she wanted, asking him all kinds of questions. I distinctly remember her mentioning a fifteen-foot pool. Just the thought of it—fifteen feet sounded enormous! My sisters, my brother, and I were all just about bursting at the seams, but Mama tried to keep us quiet as she gathered information. Well, when she started getting specific—like asking how to run the pump—the salesman turned to her and said, in no uncertain terms, "Lady, you ought to not be looking at things you can't afford." I guess he thought she was just wasting his time. He thought wrong. Mama told him, *in no uncertain terms*, that he should not presume to know what a person can and can't afford.

Mama went over to the other sales guy, the younger white guy. He answered all of her questions, one by one, and even indulged us kids. He explained everything we could have wanted to know about the pool and then some.

I don't think that Mama was actually planning to *buy* the pool that day. I think that the trip to Sears was intended to be just a shopping-around kind of trip. But she had the money and the motivation to make her point. She told the sales guy that we'd take it, right then and there. And you can bet that she made sure the other sales guy saw her making the purchase. I don't remember how many seasons that swimming pool lasted, but I'll never forget the pride on my mother's face. I'm sure that pride was twofold: partially because she knew her babies wouldn't have to swim with fish that died of who-knows-what, and partially because *she* had bought the pool that she had promised.

5

Mennonites to the Rescue

They say that truth is stranger than fiction. I guess I'd have to agree, because the story of our house being built includes a cast of some unbelievable characters. The construction got underway when Daddy was still alive, around 1965. He had this multicultural band of friends that always seemed to come and go. They helped out a lot in different ways, each with a different specialty. And when those friends were around, life in our house took on a different tone.

Daddy needed a lot of help, since he was paralyzed, but he also seemed to need people to share in his suffering. That, he had in his family. Now, of course, after the shooting, he was paralyzed from the waist down. The doctors, his therapist, everyone—they all said that he couldn't feel a thing. Well, you could've fooled us. According to Daddy, he had spasms in his legs on a regular basis… especially in the middle of the night. For some reason, these "spasms" necessitated that he call each of the six of us by name, startling us awake with his midnight yelling and screaming. He was not a big man, but he absolutely insisted that he have all six pairs of hands massaging his legs. He was so ornery, I think probably all of those nerves in his legs were probably misfiring or something. The point is that he made sure we all knew he was suffering.

I know I've said it before, but my father was not a very nice man. I don't once remember him saying please or thank you. Once the spasm of pain disappeared—or he was sufficiently satisfied that we'd all answered his beck and call—he simply dismissed us all to go to back to bed. That scenario played out over and over again until the day he died… with him cussing up a storm every step of the way.

Things were different when Dad's friends were around, especially when it came to needing their help with the house. First of all, there was Saw-Saw. He was a very large black man, at least twice my daddy's size. Mama said he used to deliver coal door-to-door, carrying heavy sacks on his back to those who had coal-burning stoves. He was the only one of my daddy's friends that we were always happy to see. Saw-Saw always arrived to our house with a happy spirit, a half-smoked, half-chewed cigar that smelled really strong, and a story for us kids. It was always the same story, but every time he came we wanted to hear him tell it. We would plead, "Saw-Saw, Saw-Saw please tell us a story!" And he was always happy to. It went like this: *"I studied. . .Alllll the starss. . . and . . .ancient Angel Anthropology. . . .went to see ol' Mo. . .shot at meeeee. . . Kill't my partna. . . should'a seen ol' granpap run. . ."* That was it! That was the whole story!! It always fed our imagination!

Then there was an Italian guy who knocked on our door within hours of Dad calling him. He was a plumber or something—Dad called him "the Dago." We had no idea it was a bad word, so every time we answered the door and saw it was him, we'd run around saying, "Hey, Daddy, it's the Dago!" Of course, that's just how he and Daddy talked to each other. Then there was also a Polish guy. Those two were part of a union or something, because any work that had to be completed to code by union workers, they got it done. They helped out Daddy a lot by getting the foundation poured and all of the plumbing and the sewer lines completed and hooked up to the city sewer lines and inspected by city. I didn't know anything about that kind of stuff. I just remember that "passing inspection" and "being up to code" were big topics in my parents' conversations about the building.

I also remember a guy named Charlie Watkins. He was a big guy, half Native-American, and under his hat he had a big, thick, long braid. He was so dark he looked black to me, but he had Indian roots in Oklahoma. He was the main bricklayer, one of only two.

All of these men were like "Johnny on the spot" for my dad. He called; they came. It was like my daddy had a whole other life outside of us. If you ask me, my daddy had mob connections. My cousin, his sister's only child, talks about that possibility, too. Supposedly Daddy knew lots of the Chicago gangsters and knew all of the ins and outs. Of course, it's all speculation, but it explains how things got done and how my dad was a different man when those guys were around—just as sweet as could be, in a way. He'd give us a quarter or a nickel or a dime and tell us to leave them be, go buy some candy and let them do their business.

Over time, Charlie Watkins and Mr. Johnson helped to slowly get the bricks laid all the way up. Again, due to some city requirement, Dad had to hire an outside contractor to get the roof done. And again Daddy's friends seemed to help out in some way. The first guy messed up, didn't do something according to the contract, so Dad got rid of him. It wasn't a big expense. Somehow Daddy seemed to "make out" on this deal and simply got another contractor to finish the job. Everything passed inspection, and that was the point when we were able to move into the basement, which was a good thing, because the old house was literally falling apart. In the winters, Mom spent a lot of time and energy just trying to patch things to keep the cold air out. So we moved into the basement of the house and built it up from there.

Once we moved in, finishing the construction was slow going. Mom worked for Motorola by then, and with each paycheck, she was able to buy a few sheets of drywall at a time. She'd bring it home, and we kids would help hold it up while she and my brother nailed it in. Dad would supervise, of course.

By the time Daddy passed away, in the spring of 1970, we had moved up out of the basement and on to the first floor. We all had bedrooms, and the kitchen was fully functional. The second floor, though, was still pretty raw. You'd go upstairs and see this big empty space. There were going to be two apartments in that space, but they had a long way to go. And I don't know if Daddy had been paying people off somehow, but that section was not up to code. By the fall of 1970, our home was in jeopardy. Every once in a while, inspectors would come by and threaten to kick us out if construction wasn't completed by a certain date.

Mama was not having any of that! She took it to prayer, like she did so many other things. We went to a Mennonite church, and my grandmother was very active in the WMSC, the Women's Missionary Service Commitee. Well, the word got out. Mama's simple prayer request for some kind of help with the house became a mission in itself. Fortunately, the Mennonites are very good at communicating through the grapevine of their fellow churches. Our plight was written up in a newsletter as the story of a widowed woman and her children who needed help to save their home and their fate, which was true!

The Mennonite Disaster Service—MDS—was an international mission service. During the winters, when they couldn't farm, Mennonites would go overseas to provide assistance to poor people in other countries. After hearing our story, word started spreading that the MDS needed to start doing work in the inner city. Well, the calls started coming in. A group from Indiana had read our story, and they were ready and willing to help. They said that if Mama could provide the materials, they would supply the labor. We had a long way to go and a short time to get there, so Mama agreed and we were on our way.

Now, this was around 1970 in inner city Chicago not far from where the business community, two blocks from our home, had been burned during the riots that erupted after Martin Luther King, Jr. was assassinated. We were an inner city, poor black neighborhood. To this day, there's an older neighbor who still talks about how odd it was to see carloads of white people—mostly men with beards and overalls—pull up to our home looking like country bumpkins, piling out with tools in hand, ready to go to work. We were so nervous. We didn't know what to do at first, how to help accommodate these people. I think the minister helped us buy donuts and this big industrial-sized coffee pot. At least we could offer them those things.

The first several crews that came were mostly men because it was generally hard construction work that had yet to be done: framing, hanging doors, installing insulation, etc. The fourth or so crew included women, who helped us out with the finishing touches: picking out paint, painting, laying the flooring, etc. They were so kind. This one church kind of took us under its wing, donating paint and other supplies. The women really helped to decorate, too. I think it was all kind of overwhelming for Mama. By the time those women were done, the front apartment was completely habitable and nice! That was important to Mama because she had always wanted to be able to provide for her parents, and now she could do so. They had a place to live:

It was quite an experience. Through all of the months that those people helped us, our church often housed them. They stayed over on cots and sleeping bags, and the church daycare center became their weekend home. They worshipped with us on Sunday morning and shared a potluck dinner after service.

The experience of completing the house became so much more than it appeared to be on the surface. As we built the house, we were sort of building a bigger life, too. The whole process gained this momentum that became sort of a cross-cultural exchange in many ways. One of the women, Berdina, ended up really befriending us. Later, Berdina would end up taking me in and giving me a home while I attended high school as part of the High Aim Program. And the country Mennonites from Indiana got to experience little windows of inner city life, too. It was a blessing for all of us in many ways, to have our lives blend in such a unique give and take. Sometimes I still can't help but wonder if Daddy was watching it all from somewhere and marveling at how we pulled it off.

The Giant Chicken

I can't even begin to imagine how different our lives would have been if not for the relationship with the Mennonites. Our relationship with the Mennonite Church started when my mom was a kid. She was probably eleven years old when she and Grandpa joined the church. So, yes, we were part of the church. Yes, they stepped in at a time when we really needed help and helped to finish building our home. But it was more than those things. It was friendship. They befriended us, and we befriended them.

One of the things that came out of the friendship with Berdina Hartman, in particular, was my re-introduction to farm life. In the Mennonite Church, there's a program called Fresh Air, in which my sisters and I had participated twice before. I had been to Wellman, Iowa and Valparaiso, Indiana. It's an opportunity for city kids to spend two weeks on a farm during the summer with a family from a fellow church. It was like an exchange program. So there I was, maybe twelve years old, this girl who knew the streets and parks of Chicago but nothing about dirt roads and rolling acres. And my sisters and I were headed for the country, the county of Elkhart, about a two-hour drive from the place we knew as home.

Maybe because I was a little older, or maybe it was because we knew these people, this trip to the country was different. This was not the Fresh Air Program, where typically you were paired with a pre-determined family, strangers, either at the train station or a church parking lot. (When you think about it, and I often have, it was quite a leap of faith for mothers to entrust their babies, as young as eight or nine, to total strangers, sight unseen.) But this time it wasn't Fresh Air. We were going to visit our *friends*, the Hartmans, for a week or two on their farm. My mom drove us there.

Now, as far as I knew at the time, it was the biggest farm in the world. Looking back, I can imagine that the Hartman family must have been pretty well off. It seemed like we drove a mile or more to the house after turning onto a fairly private road; there were only two houses and an Amish farm on that road. Once we actually entered the Hartmans' property, we realized it extended as far as we could see in either direction on one side of the road. The only neighbors were Amish, but that's another story!

The Hartmans' farm was like a little community all to itself. There were barns all over the place: barns for the tractors and all the equipment, a barn for the steer, one for chickens. The horses had their own area. There were huge silos for all the corn. And then there was Mrs. Hartman's garden; it was huge! She was growing the most delicious strawberries I'd ever had! I remember that she was always sprinkling them or spraying them with this or that to help them grow or keep out the rabbits or rodents or whatever. They were her pride and joy, and she was always irked by the mysterious culprits that got into the garden for a feast.

There was so much to do at any given moment of any given day. You seldom would have found me watching morning cartoons. Instead, I was up and off exploring early most of the time. I loved just running around and discovering new things, and on this one particular morning, I'm still not sure if I discovered the thing... or if it discovered me! One of my favorite spots to play was yet another little out-building, a shed where Mrs. Hartman kept all of her gardening stuff. Well, as I rounded a corner with my head somewhat down, I looked up to get one of the biggest surprises of my life. I probably left skid marks in the dirt.

Now I'm sure I wasn't actually face-to-face with this beast, but at the time it felt like the yellow eyes that looked back at me looked straight on! In my mind, my encounter with that thing looks like a cartoon. I swear it was the biggest chicken I'd ever seen! Scared to death, I ran off to tell everyone—and got promptly laughed at, naturally. I never saw it again, but I knew in my heart and in my head that the drumsticks that would've come off that chicken were just not normal.

Sure enough, long after we left that summer, Mrs. Hartman called mama and said they had found this monstrous chicken roaming around, one that had most likely escaped the annual spring slaughter earlier that year. Even she said it was inordinately large. She also said that she figured out it was that darn chicken that was feasting on her strawberries. Well, in retrospect, I can say it was the 70s, the decade of Miracle Gro and other wonders of science aimed at getting plants and animals to grow bigger and faster. So whether her normal feed had been supplemented with hormones or she got a little boost from the fertilizer, I don't know. But I'd bet my right arm that that giant chicken's size came from more than dried corn!

My entire life has been filled with strange encounters, wacky coincidences, and fortuitous circumstances. I guess maybe God threw that one in to give even farm life an interesting little twist!

5

THE AMISH WEDDING

Luckily for me, there was a whole other layer to my experiences on the farm with the Mennonites. When I left the city and the comfort of my mama and my brother and sisters, I never could have imagined all the things I would experience. Some of them were sad. Some were heartwarming. Some were challenging. And some were just plain funny to me.

When Mom Hartman told me that we'd all been invited to a wedding, I was probably about fifteen. I know that I had to have been at least that old because of my height. Yes, my height. You see, Mrs. Hartman was a tiny thing, only about 4'9". And me? Well, I had experienced a huge growth spurt since starting high school. I started out at an average 5'4". It must have been all of the adrenaline pumping through me with leaving my home in the city or the fresh country air filling my lungs or a combination of both. Whatever it was, I quickly sprouted to 5'10". I towered over this woman who had taken me in and by whom I felt so protected and protective of all at the same time.

She explained to me that it was an Amish wedding being held by the family across the way. Well, I was pretty excited at first. It would be another new experience for me, something I could go home on the weekend and tell Mama about while we sat at the kitchen table and caught up on every little thing over coffee.

Mrs. Hartman and I went over to their house before all of the festivities, to visit and offer our help. In retrospect, I'm sure it was probably just a friendly, neighborly thing to do, the kind of thing you do for your neighbors when you live in the country. As we walked through the door, I made sure that Mrs. Hartman stayed in close proximity. Anyway, I noticed the wedding table right away, one long table, set with simple but beautiful wedding ware and décor. I looked around for the rest of the settings and saw nothing. Coming from a large family where weddings and post-funeral gatherings meant seating and food for everyone all at once, in one big group—joyful or mourning—it seemed odd to me. Always one to speak my mind, I had just had to ask.

"So, what about this?" I said, pointing to the table. "Everyone can't sit at one table. When do you reset everything for another seating?"

"Oh, no," said the woman who seemed to be in charge of everything. "After the first seating, everyone knows to clean their plate with their bread very well." She couldn't have been more matter-of-fact about it, and I couldn't have been more shocked.

I felt Mrs. Hartman looking up at me, and I looked down at her. I don't recall how I got myself out of there, but I know it happened quickly. While part of me was truly excited about the chance to experience what an Amish wedding would be like, I told myself then and there that if didn't get in on the first seating, I was not going! I came from a big family, sure. But far be it from us to eat off of one another's plates, let alone the plates of strangers...no matter how clean the plates appeared to be after a good swipe of bread!

Well, by the time I got back there on the day of the wedding, the property was full of horses and buggies. There were lots of people around; the party had started. To me, that meant just one thing: There was no way that this outsider from Chicago was going to get in to the first round of seating at the Amish wedding. In fact, to be honest, the thought of making my presence known there scared me to death. Looking back, the protectiveness that I felt for the tiny Mrs. Hartman was probably just as much about the protection that I felt and wanted from her. I felt like a stranger in a strange land.

I walked back to the Hartmans' farm. I saw all the activity and wondered what all of those people were doing. Sure, they'd swipe their plates, but they'd also talk amongst themselves. I wondered what they were saying and how they felt. Most of all, I wondered what Mrs. Hartman would have to say when she came home. Even more than that, I wondered what that strange symbol was above the entrance to their barn! But, most of all I wondered about the stories I would have to share with Mama when I went back home.

5

MAE-BELLES AND HIGH AIM

Needless to say, the Mennonite community made a big impact on my life. I met the Hartmans when they and the rest of their Mennonite community had come to help finish building our house after my father died. I'll never forget when I met Berdina Hartman and a friend of hers. They introduced themselves as Birdie and Goldie. I thought, *Grown women can't have names like that! Those are dogs' names!* My daddy's friends had nicknames, but they were more like characters to me, anyway. Where I came from, older women didn't have nicknames. Little did I know at that time how many new doors I would walk through thanks to Birdie Hartman.

It was the early 70s. The riots of the late 60s were behind the city of Chicago, and the Mennonite Church was booming, really making efforts to build bridges between rural communities and inner city communities. That's, of course, how I had gotten involved with the Hartmans and spent time on their Indiana farm during the summer. As part of this interconnectedness, Janice, a voluntary service worker, was in charge of most youth programs at our church. She was basically doing the opposite exchange. She was from a rural community and was spending time in the inner city. Through her I learned about the High Aim program, which allowed high school age students to do a similar exchange but during the school year, not just the summer.

The program was designed through the knowledge that schools in poor communities frequently offered only substandard education. High Aim allowed inner city kids to move to different, rural areas where they could be part of smaller private schools with better curricula and more opportunities to create a foundation for college and a better life. The funny thing was, I didn't really fit the mold for the kind of student they were looking for. I wasn't exactly academically challenged and was already on a track for success. I had been selected to go to Lane Technical School, which only took the cream of the crop from schools around Chicago. However, my sister, Dimples, whose proper name was Theolane, *was* the kind of student they wanted, one who wasn't making the grade, so to speak, in the inner city school system. I don't know if it was sibling rivalry or just plain jealousy, but the idea of her getting to pack up her stuff and have some kind of great adventure away from home changed my plans for me. I decided that I, too, wanted to participate in High Aim.

Mama said okay, and off we went, Dimples to Iowa and I to Indiana. Before I explain all of the positive, life-changing events, I have to say that the transition itself was both exciting and terrifying. In 1972, the television was filled with images of the Vietnam War. I remember looking at those soldiers and thinking that I probably could relate to how they felt: alone in unknown territory. I guess Mama knew that we probably weren't as conservative as rural Mennonites, so we spent a good part of the summer getting ready for the move. I remember Mama making new clothes for us, especially skirts that were longer than we city kids were used to wearing!

Becoming a part of a new family was the hardest. I recall Mrs. Hartman telling me to just call her Berdina, but I just couldn't bring myself to call an older woman by her first name. It just felt so disrespectful. We finally compromised on Mom Hartman. While I eventually got to move into one of the upstairs bedroom (after the oldest adopted daughter dropped out of school and moved away), my first bedroom was in the basement. Now, it was very nice, don't get me wrong, and I know that there was no ill intent in it. There was simply no room for me upstairs at first. So they had partitioned a section off below. It was beautifully painted, and I had my own bookcases, but still I felt like this poor little black child who had been relegated to the basement like a puppy dog. Of course, I couldn't tell them how I felt. I just remained quiet... and upset.

For some reason that I still don't understand, I didn't talk to Mama on the phone for a long time. Maybe subconsciously I just knew I would fall apart if I did, and I was trying so hard to keep it all together. I was doing a good job of it. Everyone was so surprised when I made the Honor Roll and got my name in the newspaper. They didn't understand that I had always been a good student. I just kind of stayed under the radar and did my thing. When I finally did talk to Mama, I just absolutely broke down. Mom Hartman was so completely at a loss, trying to comfort me, but what I needed was my mama. She came to get me right away for the weekend. By the time we got home, I felt so much better. I told Mama everything was fine, really... My grades were good. I liked school, and I liked the Hartmans. It really came down to the feeling of isolation I had in the basement.

When Mama took me back to Indiana, everything changed. She came downstairs and saw my room and told Mrs. Hartman how I felt. Somehow, that made it all okay. Shortly after that, I did get to move upstairs, and then life went happily on. People were listening to me. I had a voice and people were hearing it. I landed on my feet and was off and running!

With my confidence growing, I started to think of the bigger picture of this world that I was living in. Plus, I guess maybe with being a child of the 70s, I started to see myself as kind of an activist. I looked around me at Bethany High School during my sophomore year and saw only one other black female; we two were the entire black population of my class. I realized that if Bethany, in particular, and the Mennonite Church, in general, wanted to reflect society, then a bigger percentage of their population should be African-American, just like the general population. Our class—our grade—had fifty-nine students, which meant that we should have at least five or six black students. I set my mind on recruitment!

As an honor student, I had some credibility. I talked about my idea with the principal, Levi Miller. He said, "If you can recruit them, we'll take them!" In the summer, without a job, I had nothing better to do. I recruited my sister and my cousin back in Chicago. I also enlisted the help of Leavette, one of the other girls who was already there with me. She, in turn, recruited Christine. I also recruited Valerie, my next-door neighbor back in Chicago. Christine, Valerie and I became the MAE-Belles—but I'll save that for later in the story. The point is that having an African-American group of students, empowered all of us, I think. It certainly did me.

We were all very different. Christine was a singer and an actress. She preferred to be called Kit, but didn't like the spelling. This became one of our first intellectual missions together. It probably happened over lunch one day, early in our junior year, as we were getting to know one another. The four of us were discussing it. She wanted to spell "Kit" with a Q. At first, we all thought, *You can't do that.* We explored the dictionary, which revealed that "Q" was almost always followed by a "u". Hmm, a dilemma. After all, "Quit" would not work! So it had to be "Qit." We took it to our English teacher, Everett Thomas, to whom I must in part dedicate this work. He confirmed what we had already learned. There was no written rule about it. After much discussion together, Christine decided that it was her name and she had the right to spell it with a "Q" without using a "u". In fact, she reserved the right to spell it any way she wanted. We all agreed. That is how Kit became Qit, and we had a practical experience in self-empowerment.

Anyway, like I was saying, Qit was a singer and actress. She found acting in high school and was a vocalist in her Mennonite church's youth band. I don't recall the name, but it was real band, with drums, bass and guitar. I recall that she did a bang up job as the stage manager in the school production of *Our Town.* Meanwhile, Val was really outgoing, bright, articulate, and rebellious. She couldn't sing, but she liked the drama department and joined Qit in the plays and stuff. She was the only one with a secular background, so she was always voicing perspectives that she knew would shock people in this "church" school. Leavette was always sort of quiet. Me? I was the much more conservative, studious one; the organizer, the motivator. I was the only one who took four years of math and science. I finally had to take a class at the local college in order to get into a pre-calculus class! Leavette and Qit were both petite, about 5'2". Val was probably about 5'7". I towered over all of them!

It was so funny. As a group, we black kids went from being on the fringe to being the coolest kids at school. Everyone wanted to be friends with the black kids! We had the cool music. We were just a dynamic group, in general. We hung out together in the lunchroom. The faculty tried to dissuade us from congregating, asking us to inter-mingle more, but we liked each others' company and the white kids came to us, anyway, even though there was some tension when we were all together. Val made friends with a couple of Canadian guys, and they were really cool with us. It was just such a great time. I remember how much I sort of grew into my own style then. I had an Afro, and there was no way that the traditional little Mennonite cap was going to fit on my head! It looked like one of those little Jewish yamakas! We called them beanies or "crash helmets". Both Mama and Mom Hartman were great seamstresses, so I learned to sew a lot of my own skirts and bell-bottoms and knit tops. But I hated jeans!

One of my fondest memories is that we started this certain group. I spurred it on because our history book at the time was so outdated. It still had Eisenhower as President and said nothing about black people except that we were slaves. I took issue with it with our teacher. He was a pretty cool guy and told me to come up with something. That something was The Black Awareness Group. Our goal was to focus on the modern history of African-Americans. So we started with the mid-70s and the Black Panther Party. The teacher was fully supportive and even intrigued. We kept it going, engaged in great dialogue, and brought books—a variety of paperbacks—about the Black Panthers. We all learned more than we bargained for, too, because all of our parents tried to keep us away from militant stuff.

Well, interest grew and before we knew it, we extended our con-versations into lunchtimes. We had met this one college student, Arvis, who needed to do some student teaching or something. We went to meet him to bring him in to lead our group, and I'll never forget when we met him; he had one of the biggest Afros I had ever seen and wore a Mickey Mouse watch on a bus driver wristband. He thought we were college students, at first, which is pretty cool when you're only sixteen. So, since we thought he was so cool, we figured he would be a good leader for us. The Black Awareness Group became a forum for discussing the issues of the day and expanded to become a cross-cultural exchange. Although the school and the group were predominantly white, through the smattering of Black, Hispanic, Puerto Rican, and foreign exchange students, we all reaped the benefits of getting to see multiple issues from differing points of view. We started off as a group of ten but eventually filled an entire classroom.

The conversations got pretty diverse. We talked about leaders like Kennedy and Lincoln and the legalization of marijuana. Again, Val had the secular background, so she was always able to offer the worldly, sometimes racy opinion. She thought marijuana should be legalized, for example. I always took the counter-position. We were both pretty strong, influential personalities. So it went with discussions about abortion and politics, too. It was great, really, because we could start off on a benign subject and end up seeing the controversy in it. Still and all, the dialogue was always respectful.

I had some great times in high school. We all had the similar experience of doing our best to fit in and simultaneously retain our identities in a world that was distinctly different than the one we had come from. I remember how, when we first came to town, we got a lot of stares—not pretty ones—especially from the children. Many Amish people were blonde with blue eyes, and many Mennonites were dark haired. Regardless, because they did not have televisions, brown-skinned people were new to many of the young people. I eventually had to learn how to stare right back! I remember Val and Qit telling stories of the things they encountered on their bike rides. One time, they were nearly run off the road by some man in a car. But we didn't focus on those things when there were so many other good experiences.

One such experience started off as typical high school fun but ended up with me having to take a stand again. Val and I had convinced another girl to let us use her car to skip school one afternoon and go the mall. Now, it didn't occur to me at the time that two of the few black girls at school missing at the same time would be noticed. Besides, while Val had skipped school before, it was a first time for me and I didn't know what to expect. We had fun and got back to school in time go on our merry way, or so we thought.

We didn't get called in to the office until the next day. For Val, it was no big deal; the principal didn't come down on her too hard. For me, it was a different story. "How could you do such a thing? You're a role model!" It was such a big deal. I was so angry.

My biggest gripe, and maybe part of my motivation, had been this: I wasn't there to be a role model for anybody else. I wasn't very well liked at school because I was so smart, the "honor roll student." The principal trying to put me on a pedestal as an "example to the black students" while I already stood out just wasn't working. So, I changed it. As a junior, I finally felt like I was part of group. Val, Christine, Leavette and I were ready to make our way through high school as part of a bigger, growing group.

I answered the principal quite eloquently. "If this is the debt I owe you for allowing me to be here, this debt is far greater than I can pay." He looked at me blankly, not knowing what I meant. Again, he was trying to put me on a pedestal, someplace I did not want to be. I told him if he kept holding me above my friends, I would soon have no friends left. I left his office and walked home. By then I was staying with another family, the Yoders. I packed a bag and asked to be driven to the bus station. Before the principal even knew what was happening, I had dropped out and was back in Chicago. I told Mama I was quitting, that I could no longer go there.

I didn't know what I was going to do. Lane, the tech school I was supposed to go to originally, was no longer accepting students. My only option was John Marshall. Well, I went there one day to visit and knew I just couldn't do it. It was old, like the high school in *Lean on Me*. There were literally chains on the door. Every other light bulb was out, and graffiti was all over the walls. Chaos was everywhere. I was used to Bethany: small, bright, peaceful, and just over a decade old.

Fortunately, later that week, Mama got a call from Principal Miller. He was concerned because no one knew where I was. He apologized for the way he'd come down on me and for not calling sooner. Mama told him, "You don't have to apologize to me! You have to apologize to Annette!" You see, Mama was supportive. While I had definitely done the wrong thing by ditching school, she knew that I was a good student and told me I had far exceeded anything she had accomplished in school. She knew that I would be successful, and she told me she could no longer help me, which gave me the freedom to make my decision. When I got on the phone with Mr. Miller, he apologized for putting me in the position he had, and I admitted to my collusion. I went back to Bethany, but with a stronger, better perspective of who I was and what I wanted my role to be.

Somehow, through those years of being away from home, of having to find my way and make my way, I had found—and was continuing to find—my voice. It was a combination of things, really. I spent many weekend evenings at home with Mama talking late into the night after she got home from her late shift. Our time was precious. The immediacy of it all made me want to take full advantage of it. I felt the same when I was with Mom Hartman. I recall having one very poignant conversation with her about race and religion. It probably was a result of her daughters meeting my brother; they went sort of "gaga" and Mom Hartman was clearly uncomfortable. Meanwhile, Mama had warned me not to come home with a white boyfriend. When I asked Berdina about the issue, she hemmed and hawed. I finally asked if she would rather one of her adopted daughters marry a white Roman Catholic or a black Mennonite. Through tears, she finally admitted that she would prefer a white Roman Catholic. I didn't think much of it at the time, but I see now that it was a very frank conversation for a teenager to have with a middle-aged woman. Regardless, I respected her for being honest with me. Conversations like these helped to build the faith that I had in myself and to refine my seemingly innate ability to draw people out of themselves.

Anyway, I was glad to be back with my friends at Bethany. I had actually known Val for a long time. We'd been neighbors since my family had moved into the new house when I was ten years old. When I recruited her to Bethany, she had already had problems at her high school for telling off a teacher. She, too, had been on her way to John Marshall. Thank God we both escaped that fate!

We've all remained friends, especially Qit, Val, and I. After high school, Val went on to become a model; hence the "M" in MAE-belles. She moved to Milan where her career blossomed. Qit became an actress; hence the "A" in MAE-belles. She opted to go to work for the Chocolate Chip Theater in Chicago. Much later, I remember taking my son to see a play she did. I went on to college, earned my bachelors degree, and became an engineer; hence the "E" in MAE-belles.

When we were all in our mid 30s, I moved back to Chicago. I was fixing up Mom's basement and trying to figure out the next chapter of my life. Val had returned from Italy. Qit had always stayed in Chicago. We all got together again and talked about how the intertwining of our lives would make a good story. We could call it the MAE-Belles, the Story of the Model, the Actress, and the Engineer. I had recently seen *The Women of Brewster Place* and thought that our story would be much more exciting!

Through all of the ups and downs, I've wondered what kept me on the straight and narrow all of those years and beyond. There's one particular incident that comes to mind in that regard. When I was about seven or eight years old, Mom and Dad were off somewhere, maybe to therapy, and we kids were home with Donna and my brother in charge. While we were all horsing around, my sister broke Mama's favorite lamp. It was a black stallion with gold trim painted on it. I've seen them a million times since then at swap meets and Good Will stores; I guess it was a classic lamp of the 60s. Well, my sister was a mean one. She threatened us, so we were all afraid to tell who had done it. Her logic was that if nobody told, nobody would get in trouble. Her logic was flawed. Mama decided that if nobody told, *everybody* would get in trouble. She made us all lean over the bed with our bare butts showing. To add to the agony, she took a cigarette break before coming and beating us all with Daddy's leather belt. She did it not once but twice; we got two beatings, with a break in between!

By the second time, I had made up my mind. I told myself I would never get beaten like that again. I was crying, knowing that I was innocent and made a conscious decision to never again let myself get punished for something I didn't do. And while I was it I would avoid doing anything worth getting punished for in the first place! I never got a whooping again. Aside from some momentary lapses, I've kept that resolve, and it's served me well. I think I learned in those days how to be the voice of a group while helping a group to find its own voice… instead of suffering in silence.

MY SPECIAL RELATIONSHIP
WITH MAMA

I guess there were a lot of things that contributed to the special relationship that Mama and I had and continue to have. She loved us all, but she always told me I was special. Of course, there had been the issue of her thinking that I would be the child she'd lose; when that didn't come to pass, I think she really drew me close to her emotionally. It was more than that, though. Our relationship had a dynamic born of both inherent qualities and simple circumstances. Whatever the myriad reasons, I'm glad for them.

One of those circumstances formed during the course of my high school years, when I lived away from home as part of the High Aim program. When I did come home on weekends and holidays and semester breaks, our time together was special, and we treasured it. We no longer had the typical mother/daughter relationship. That is, I wasn't around day in and day out for her to be on my case and me to be on her nerves. We spent hours and hours up late at night, just sitting at the kitchen table talking and getting to know each other in ways that most mothers and daughters probably don't ever get to experience. Mama always sat in the same place; it was like the one little area of the house that was hers alone, at the south end of the kitchen table, facing north. You could see into the living room from there, get an idea of who was coming and going. Even long after high school, well into the 90s, I remember sitting in the kitchen, with Mama sitting in what had been Daddy's spot when he was alive, and just talking with her for hours.

I got to know Mama's life story from high school to marriage to babies to everything. On the flip side, I guess you could say that I didn't see my family through the same rose-colored glasses that my siblings did, especially my brother. I did, however, get to see a fuller side of my mother and—by extension—my family and myself, so I'm not complaining.

The fact that my father was no longer around, I'm sure, contributed to Mama and I growing close. It's hard to have friends, much less nurture relationships of any kind with your family, when you have a mean old husband yelling and calling you names every time you turn around. So I think that Mama was probably able to let her guard down a bit after Daddy died. At least, it felt like that to me. My father had always demanded a lot of attention in my early years. He died when I was twelve, so Mama probably got to know my siblings and me in ways she never would've had he lived longer.

By the time I started high school, most of Mama's friends—or women who would have been her friends had my father allowed her to do anything—simply were not very close and had moved on. So, again, my trips home were a chance for her to be social. And in my sophomore year, Mama confided in me just how smart she thought I was, how I had the potential to do better than anything she had imagined for herself. She also told me she couldn't help me, that I was on my own, but that she had utmost faith in me and would do whatever she could to support my efforts. Mama respected me, and that meant a lot to both of us.

Some of our most poignant conversations revolved around my sister Donna. I think in many ways, I related most to Donna before I ever understood why. You see, she and I were the dark-complexioned ones in the family. My brother and middle sister were light-complexioned. And so it went that they were the favored ones in the extended family. They both got special treatment and gifts sometimes from Aunt Ernestine and Grandma Bubba. Donna was also very smart, and after she died, I figured that if I wanted favorable attention, it had to come from being smart. I couldn't change the color of my skin, but I could apply myself and do extremely well in school… and I did just that. I recall early on helping my older sister, Dimples, learn to read. She was probably what you would today call dyslexic, although there was no name for it back then. I didn't think about the color issues when I felt smart. I think that Mama always felt for me in that way.

5

The color issue was an interesting one that came into my full awareness during those high school years and those talks with Mama. Her father was actually Cuban, which somewhat accounted for Mama's lighter skin and beautiful, wavy hair. In fact, I remember shopping in the Hispanic neighborhoods with her, and the cashiers would always speak to her in Spanish. Of course, as a kid, I knew that my grandfather had an interesting accent, but that was as far as it went in my mind for a long time. Then, one time on a trip home during my freshman year, I remember looking at him and thinking, *My grandfather is not black!* That was the term back then; now it's politically correct to say African-American, I guess. Anyway, it was a turbulent time—late 60s, early 70s—and race and skin color were at the forefront of so many issues that touched my life. Regardless of the mixed bloodlines, Mama has always been proud of being a black woman and has always identified herself as such. In all of our conversations, it was never really an issue for her and so it never became one for me, either.

Her pride did, though, extend to a distaste for interracial marriage. Now, as far as I could tell, she didn't have hard feelings toward either of her parents, so her strong feelings were kind of confusing for us kids. We even laughed about it sometimes, reminding her that she was the product of a mixed marriage. But, true to form, Mama would not budge on the subject. In fact, when I went away to school, she told me outright, "Keep your dress down, your panties up... and don't bring home any white boys! I'm sending you to school to get an education, and that's all I want you to get!" She was very straightforward! It always sent her into a bit of a tailspin when I would bring home friends from school for the weekend. Of course, there weren't many black students at my school, so many of my friends were white. As time went by, Mama was afraid that my female friends would start hanging out with male counterparts, which meant that I would gravitate to their *other* white friends. Time and again I assured Mama there at that kitchen table that she had no need to worry.

One time, though, she did tell me another story that shed some light on her stance. Come to find out, my mother's grandmother hadn't been born into slavery but shortly after the time of Emancipation. I guess that's probably not much of a surprise, actually, given that she was born around the late 1860s and lived in this country. Her name was Mary Jane Bell, and she was the product of rape by a white man. Well, as the story goes, when her father came to see her, she ran away from home because she never wanted to meet the man who had done these horrible things to her mother. We have pictures of her; she looked like a little old white lady.

She and my mother were very close. Mama, of course, heard about all of her horrible feelings for this white man. As a result, Mary Jane married the darkest man she could. Conley L. Henderson was just as African as he could be and was an AME minister in the early years of the church. Naturally, a lot of Mama's feelings about interracial marriages come from her grandmother's life. When you have an awareness of where you come from, who you come from, and what the circumstances were, sometimes that awareness is not kind to you and does not lend any happiness to your life. I suppose maybe my mama was able to talk to her grandmother like I've always been able to talk with her. Sitting at the table in those wee hours of the night gave me insight into so much more than Mama's life alone.

When it comes right down to it—through all of the conversations we had through the years—our talks really began with a deep sort of longing pain in me that begged for an answer. Finally, I asked it. I had never seen any baby pictures of me. They simply didn't exist. I wanted to know why. It seemed like Mama really needed to think about that one for a bit. She finally told me that the only thing she could think of was the fact that they simply weren't taking the standard newborn pictures in the hospital then…which made no sense because there were plenty of pictures of my brother and two older sisters. The earliest pictures of me, meanwhile, were taken when I was about 2½ years old.

To this day, three of my siblings' baby pictures are lined up on a shelf above my mama's bed. My brother must have been a throwback to my great-grandmother, because he was born with blondish hair and blue eyes. The lady next to her in the maternity ward thought they'd brought her the wrong baby! Of course, his features eventually changed to sandy brown hair and hazel eyes. My sisters all had these cute little almond-shaped, slanted eyes; they looked like China doll babies with wavy hair. I always looked at those pictures and wondered what mine would've looked like and why they simply weren't there.

Well, through the years, my mind played out all kinds of possibilities. I don't know what possessed me to do so, but one time I actually asked my father what I looked like as a baby. "Oh, you was an ugly baby," was his reply. He went on to add that I looked like a little black Bozo the Clown, bald on top with fuzz that stood out on the sides. (Sometimes he bordered on cruel!) After that, I thought that maybe there weren't any pictures of me because I wasn't as pretty as the other ones. By the time I was sixteen years old, that thought was very traumatic to me. Or maybe I was adopted, I told myself. Then the strangest thing happened: Between the beginning of the school year and Thanksgiving break I sprouted from 5'3" to 5'10". I came back home taller than everyone! Well, I guess that got Mama thinking. She was racking her brain, admitting that I really did look different than everyone else. She even talked about how my head was bigger and shaped differently than the rest of the kids'.

It took some time, but Mama started really confiding in me, telling me things that I know she never shared with my siblings. To begin with, Mama endured the birth of her children alone. Her husband drove her to the front entrance, and she literally walked herself into the hospital. That's the kind of relationship they had. My grandparents would go there to the Presbyterian Hospital, but otherwise Mama had no one, and the first time she held each of us, there was no husband by her side, he was always working.

Well, one time when I asked her why I was so different, the story went deeper. She said she looked up at me and saw Mr. Benjamin— the man who, she said, could have actually been my father. She said that she had fallen in love with him. He had been a schoolteacher of hers years before, and she went with him one time. Just one time.

I guess she never really thought about it until I kept persisting with my questions, but when she did the math, she realized that maybe, just maybe the timing made sense. When she found out she was pregnant, she assumed it was her husband's child and knew for certain that she couldn't see Mr. Benjamin again. So, at that point, with this realization and all of our candid talks, she contacted him. At that point, my father had been dead for years, and Mr. Benjamin was married. I don't know what else they said to one another, but I do know that it was followed by a strange occurrence.

Some time later, when I was in college, a strange man approached me while I was waiting at a bus stop during my commute. I don't really remember the details. He came out of nowhere and started a conversation. He was very curious about me, very friendly. It caught me totally off guard, and strangers were always sort of suspect to me, anyway. When I told Mama about it, she asked me what the man looked like. When I told her, she said, "That was probably Mr. Benjamin." At first I said, "What are you talking about?" because I would never have put two and two together like that.

The whole thing was so confusing for me. I remember that I had always looked up to my mother. I have this picture in my mind that I've had of her since I was about six years old. It's her in this black trench coat that she used to wear. She always stood so tall and stately. Sometimes she would catch me just staring up at her and ask me, "Why do you look up at me like that?" I would say, "You walk so tall and straight; you look like a school teacher. I wanna grow up to be just like you." Well, when she first told me about her love affair, I just rejected those feelings, at least on the surface. Of course, she had tried to date now and then after our father died, but—as kids generally try to do—we chased off any possible suitors. Kids are protective of their moms, you know. I guess I felt no different about the thought of her and Mr. Benjamin, especially since I was brought into the issue. I wanted nothing to do with the idea and actually told her, "You're just a lonely old widow woman." I told myself that she was just lost in the longing of a fantasy, of a life she could have had but chose not to. On the one hand, I felt sort of honored that Mama had confided in me and that she felt I was mature enough to handle the news. On the other hand, I resented having to bear what I considered a nebulous burden. I mean, I couldn't tell anyone, couldn't run around saying,

"Mama thinks I'm someone else's child!"

Ultimately, I never really believed it. I just accepted the choices that Mama had made, regardless of how they played out. My years have given me the perspective that life just is what it is... and what you make it. And my mama was more than my mother; she was a woman unto herself, too.

Years later, I decided to track down my roots, to learn something about my father's family. While on a business trip, I took a little side venture to Louisiana. One connection led to another. Before I knew it, I was standing in the doorway of a man who swore up and down that I was one of his cousins. He said I looked just like the Brittons. My son, the rest of my family, and I have been to numerous family reunions since then, with people who look a lot like me. But that's material for another story.

As for the baby pictures that never were, I've accepted the fact that I'll never know what I looked like as a baby. With three children already—and a mean old cuss of a husband—Mama probably had almost more on her plate than she could handle by the time I came along. By the time my father died, she was only thirty-five years old. She probably hadn't paused for a deep breath in all of those previous years with him. In retrospect, I can see that Mama changed, opened up, relaxed in many ways when our long, late night talks began. I know that we both looked forward to them and that we will both always treasure them. I think that she has lived with a broken heart for a long, long time, the pieces of it held together by all of the time and effort that she put into her family. Recently, she held my hand while I sat beside her hospital bed. She told me how happy she was that I was there. *Me too,* I thought. *Me too.*

ENGINEERING SCHOOL

I was an odd high school student. Again, I had always loved the library, and that fact didn't change for me even as a teenager. Of course, in high school there are always different clubs you can join. By the end of my freshman year, I was a member of the Student Librarian Club. I was surrounded by so much information all the time. I spent hours and hours researching all of the possibilities for what my college years might hold. Before I had even started my sophomore year, I knew exactly where I wanted to go to college.

I learned about summer programs offered by a couple of the universities that had my interest. I had always dreamed of becoming a doctor, so I spent part of one summer at Indiana University, which had a program catering to minorities interested in health professions. I was also just simply a math and science person, and Northwestern University had a great summer program and a strong engineering department. I did both of those programs during the summer of my junior year. They were both scholarship-based, and I always had the grades to qualify for things like that. Ultimately, Northwestern became my top pick.

My challenge was that I wasn't coming from a public high school. I was coming from Bethany, my Mennonite high school. We had guidance counselors to help us, and they were wonderful when it came to information on private colleges like Goshen College and Eastern Mennonite College. When it came to secular schools, though, my counselor couldn't help me. But in my gut, I knew that what those smaller colleges had to offer me just wouldn't be enough.

Luckily, at Goshen, I had developed a relationship with this one black professor. His name was Leroy Berry, and he suggested the University of Chicago. Well, long story short, I did all the paperwork, all the filing... and got accepted to both University of Chicago and Northwestern University.

5

I was torn, didn't know what decision to make. I had fallen in love with Northwestern during my time in the summer programs as one of their National High School Institute students. Participating in that makes you a "Cherub," and you are in good standing with the University for *life*. But I had also taken the tour of the U of C campus and fell in love with Chicago, too. I had never seen Hyde Park before, and just the fact that there was this whole campus on the south side of Chicago—in the city that I'd grown up in but never seen before—fascinated me.

I also found out that Northwestern also had an Honors Med. Program. I was excited about that possibility and applied for the program. When I didn't get accepted, my pride was hurt, and I was even more confused. There were so many confusing, complicating factors. In all of the uncertainty, I missed the deadline for Northwestern and, by default, ended up at the University of Chicago. I figured it was just the way it was supposed to be.

I was one of a small number of black students accepted that year. I recall taking a sort of introductory tour. The guide showed us all around this large, intimidating campus. The most remarkable thing I remember is them showing us where to go to speak with a counselor if we felt overwhelmed by the stress of the environment and our studies. They were very polite, but they were certain to mention that the suicide rate for undergraduates was very high. I was very surprised by that fact. I mean, U of C was renowned for their graduate programs, but I couldn't imagine that kind of stress as an undergrad.

Well, I made it through one year. My grades suffered tremendously. I'd never been challenged like that before. I was very confident but took some classes that I shouldn't have attempted right away, like upper level physics, and failed miserably. For academic and other reasons, I just became very disillusioned with the University. I never felt like I fit in there.

Sure enough, I transferred to Goshen College. When I applied, they accepted me right away. Walking on to that campus felt like old home week. Goshen was a small town, and I already had so many friends there from high school. I was still pre-med. It was the beginning of the spring semester, the dead of winter in January in Indiana. For the purpose of getting settled in, Mama had let me borrow her brand new 1977 Ford Thunderbird. On the drive there, the snow was falling and the roads were icy in spots. Of all times for it to happen, it was during that drive that I had the first car wreck of my life, just fifteen miles from the campus. I slid on some ice and that was it. The front of end of Mama's car was banged up pretty badly.

Needless to say, between waiting for the police and then waiting while they wrote up the report and everything, I arrived late to Goshen. I knew exactly where the black student housing was. I was still a bit shaken as I walked there. I'll never forget, though, what happened once I was sitting there, waiting to get all settled in. This guy walked in the room. I had no idea who he was, but when our eyes first met, I swear I saw lightning… little sparks and stars all over the place, like electricity. His name was Michael. He was kind of cute, an international student from Belize. I had never had that kind of feeling before in my entire life. The attraction was immediate, and we became fast friends.

There were actually a lot of international students there, from Belize, Haiti, Honduras, Somalia and South America. I enjoyed being friendly and outgoing, over time acquired the nickname "The Breeze," because I was always on the move, breezing in and out. I guess I was sort of an ambassador. I always had a lot of friends and was always introducing people, sort of the go-between. It seemed like there was always a card game or something going on in the "Black House," as we called it, but I could never bring myself to participate, never sit still that long. I was social, but kept myself on the periphery of many things because ultimately, I was a very serious student, and my studies simply meant more to me.

Still, I loved communicating across lines of people. Some of the best times I had in college were when I moved off-campus. My friend Yolanda (she was Puerto Rican) moved into a house with an upperclassman; I think she was Canadian. Together, we threw one of the best multicultural off-campus parties that there had ever been. Everyone commented on how they had such a great time partying together—blacks, whites, Puerto Ricans, you name it. Such parties were usually cliquish, especially at this Christian college. Well, we were having none of that at our party! We got everybody up to dance together, and when we started the soul-train line, every person there was a part of it!

Again, I really attribute my being able to interact with people, draw them out, and motivate them toward a common goal of any kind to the time that I spent with Mom Hartman overcoming my shyness. Those experiences that I had away from home in the Mennonite community really helped to draw me out of myself. I feel, in some ways, like helping to draw other people out has been the natural trickle down effect.

In high school and college, when four or five of us black students were sitting together, interacting with each other and enjoying ourselves, it really bothered me that somehow it was frowned upon by the administration. It was as though they were uncomfortable when we black students just hung out together, but it was okay when they congregated together. I found myself many times joining little groups and just starting a dialogue and bringing other people into it. It didn't matter about the subject so much. We would just talk about anything that was going on in the world. It was all about the interaction!

Speaking of interaction brings me back to the broken heart story. I think everybody has at least one, here's mine. I had these two girl-friends, Gail and Sarah. Sarah and I had gone to high school together. Gail and I met there at Goshen. We had a great cross-cultural friend-ship on a very personal level. I confided in them about my feelings for Michael. He lived off-campus, too, and I loved throwing parties at the house where he lived with his Somali friends. I always provided the music. I brought Gail and Sarah into the circle of friends, including Michael.

Well, that first summer I stayed there at Goshen and worked in the factory to help pay for my schooling. During the summer of heartbreak, though, I went home to Chicago to work. When I came back, I couldn't wait to see Michael. The moment he answered the door, I just knew I was in the middle of something that felt odd. He was polite, and on the surface everything looked fine. It was just the feeling I had. A week or so later, Gail came by my little apartment. She explained to me that Sarah had been there with Michael when I had gone to visit. When she realized that it was me at the front door, she ran out the back door. So much for my friendship with Sarah, and so much for the friendship with Michael that I wanted to be more.

Sarah and Michael ended up marrying. I don't know if it was for love or for a green card, it really doesn't matter, but there was alot of that going on at the time. Ultimately, most of the international students wanted to marry to stay in the country and continue their studies and pursue careers. One of my friends, Lloyd, around the same time, asked me if I would marry him so that he could continue his education. I told him, "No, I just couldn't do that." It was just the wrong reason in my mind. He was fine with my answer, and we went on to a party that evening, never really thinking much of it. In the meantime, though, my heart was just broken by the loss of my friend Michael and saddened by the loss of my friend Sarah. And we never, ever spoke about it. It was a friendship lost.

I called my mother, of course. At that time, I was so distraught about several of the things on my plate. I had made it through a year and a half there. All of a sudden, though, I found myself facing a big commitment; as a pre-med student, I had to get ready to take the MCATS. The stress of preparing for those tests was compounded by the fact that, as my mother said, I was also suffering from a broken heart. "Well, Annette, maybe you should just come home," she told me. Wow! In all the years since I had first left home, my mother had never said that. They were the most soothing, comforting, loving words I had ever heard. So, that semester, the beginning of my junior year, I withdrew from all my classes, packed my bags, and headed back home to Chicago. I just didn't feel right continuing on a path I wasn't sure about. I didn't know if I'd qualify for scholarships. I didn't want to start something I might not finish, and I just plain hurt inside.

The first order of business was to make some money. I knew that Motorola paid pretty well because Mama had worked there for years. I started working in the factory full time doing inventory of tiny electronic parts. I had never made a full-time income before, and I enjoyed the money. Still, after about six months, I knew I couldn't continue on in something that felt like a dead end to me. I knew I had to get my degree. I didn't know what I was going to do.

It turned out that coming home was a blessing in many ways. I came home from work one day, and my brother kind of started giving me a hard time. He had been looking into DeVry Institute. He had the information he needed to start goading me. He told me, "If you're so smart and going to be pre-med, why not study engineering?" Looking back, I'm sure that his challenge was well-intended. He was probably trying to give me the kick in the pants that I needed. Of course, you had to take an entry test to get into the program, so he challenged me to take it. "If you're that smart, you should be able to get into this program."

"I know I can!" I said.

"Well, I dare you to go over there and take the test and see because I don't believe you can get in!" He gave me the ultimate challenge.

I went there, took the test, and aced it, of course. I had more math and science credits than most people taking that test because it was designed as an undergrad program, and I already had three years of college under my belt. My short experience at Motorola gave me a new perspective on things. I knew that what I really needed was a marketable skill. When I started to take a look at salaries in the field of engineering combined with the literature that DeVry was sending me, it all started to come together. It didn't hurt that with their program, I would have my Bachelor's Degree in three years. I could then go on and get my Master's Degree in biomedical engineering, if I wanted, but in the meantime, their job placement services were outstanding.

The spring of 1980 found me enrolled in the summer session at DeVry. They accepted a lot of my existing credits and offered me a great financial aid package. I really owe my brother thanks for that move! If not for his dare, I would never have even considered DeVry an option.

Frankly, I was relieved not to have to take classes like history and geography. Just give me logic; give me math and science and I would be happy! And that's what I got at DeVry. It all came very naturally to me. It was very hands-on. We went into the lab and built circuits right away. We had book study, lecture, and lab, so it all came together and made sense. During my first few years there they were seeking full accreditation. Which meant that you had to take a certain amount of general education classes, but I didn't mind that. I was fully into the meat of the engineering courses by then.

The strangest part for me was being one of very few women in the program. The race issue didn't matter; there were plenty of black guys in the program. It was more of a gender issue. There were usually thirty seats in every classroom, and each one of them was occupied. Of those thirty people, I was frequently the only woman in the class. There were two other women in the program. One was an older woman, a former nurse who had gone back to school, and one was a young girl, right out of high school. Then there was me, somewhere in the middle of that gamut.

It was hard to fit in for a while. There were definite cliques of people who formed study groups. I was always sort of odd-one-out, though. It didn't help that, once again, I worked as a student librarian on campus. It was great for solo-study time, but not so great for connecting with the other students. That kind of camaraderie finally came around for me after three or four semesters. I got a work-study job and worked there in the lab at school. I ended up working over 30 hours a week and kept up with a full school schedule, too. But being in the lab helped me to keep up with studying and helped me to get to know some of the guys. Some of them were okay, but most of them seem threatened by me. I never got invited to join their study groups.

Some of them even found ways of getting copies of whatever test might be coming up, whether it was through an inside connection or a friend who had taken the class before. Well, they never shared that information with me, even when I asked! It would have been dishonest, though, so it was all for the best. I was pretty much on my own. It always amazed me though, how much effort people put in to trying to cheat when they could've just spent the time studying the darn

material in the first place!

Once, I was sort of indirectly accused of being at the school for less than honorable academic reasons. It didn't take them long to realize though, that I was a serious student and not just a woman in a man's environment or—worse yet—a woman looking for a man in a likely place. I remember telling them, "I wouldn't be studying so hard or spending that kind of money just to hook up with one of you numbskulls!" And they definitely weren't pulling the kind of grades I was pulling, and they knew it. Some of them, in fact, were really struggling.

Many of the men in the program were pretty arrogant until DeVry got accredited. All of a sudden, a lot of these guys were overwhelmed by the idea that they had to write term papers for English classes. Then the tables were deliciously turned. All of a sudden, I was the one in demand. I don't even know how many times I heard, "Annette, would you write me a paper?" I guess after three or four semesters, I had started to earn their respect. I recall this one guy trying to engage me in a conversation about the subject of my term paper. When I explained and then turned the question to him, the truth came out and he asked me for a favor for a change. I toyed with him and loved every minute of it. "Hmmmm… What's it worth to you?" I asked. He offered me one hundred dollars, which was probably about what I made at my library job in a week.

Well, I hemmed and hawed and baited him along for a while. When I felt like he had stretched about as far as he could, I delivered the sucker punch: I told him it would really cost him, but I could certainly do it!

"How much? How much?" He couldn't wait for my offer.

"You know what, I can do this for you. I can see how this can work… but if I'm willing to give up my paper and risk plagiarism, risk getting kicked out, then I would have to be doing it for a sizeable sum of money. Exactly a full semester's tuition." Tuition was about twelve hundred dollars a semester. His face almost hit the ground. I continued, "Had you shared with me along the way I might have been able to give you a discount. But you weren't sharing information earlier with me, so you have to pay full price." With that I turned and walked away. I figured that was payback for messing up the grading curve *and* leaving me out of everything.

I studied harder in engineering school than I ever had to study in my entire life previously. In fact, while it's standard practice to sell back your books and get a portion of the money back out of them, there were a lot of books that I kept as mementos for the particularly hard classes. And I worked hard to stay afloat financially, too. Even with the number of hours that I worked through that program, I was more than $18,000 in debt when all was said and done. In the 80s, that was a lot of college debt.

My brother and sisters got a smattering of an education, a few classes, but I was the first and only one in my family to complete college. After moving back to Chicago, I lived with my family for a while. But life at home was what life at home was. Mama's house was a busy place with people coming and going all the time. I tried to hang in there and use the library and the labs for studying, but after my first semester, I knew I just had to move on. And so I did. In some ways, I feel like I've been on the move ever since.

5

THE STORY OF MAMA JO

Mama has always asked me where I get my big ideas from and wondered how I've had the guts and the determination to speak up for myself. Well, I think I came by it pretty naturally. While my Mama, Mama Jo—her actual name is Jonetta—couldn't have known what she was setting in motion at the time, it was her gumption that actually brought her and my father together and ultimately resulted in what I know as my family.

Mama Jo was a talented young seamstress. Under the tutelage of the sewing circle in the Mennonite church she attended, she had cultivated skills beyond most of her peers. She knew that she sewed well, and when she enrolled in a Home Economics class at Lucy Flowers High School, she looked forward to the sewing projects.

It soon became clear that sewing at church and sewing at school would be very different experiences. Lucy Flowers was basically an "all-white" girls' school. Now, Mama Jo looked more Italian or Hispanic than African American. She definitely wasn't a Caucasian girl, and that seemed to be the problem.

She completed her first sewing project, did well, and turned it in on time. Some of the other girls did not even finish theirs, but they all got higher grades. Mama Jo was not going to let that injustice slip by her; she decided to confront her teacher. Mama Jo was a spunky girl, but she would never have cursed or sworn. According to my niece, she called the teacher a "dried up old so-and-so"!

The teacher had quite another story. She claimed that this girl, my mother, had threatened her life! Before Mama Jo knew it, she was taken to the principal's office and then called down to the police station because the teacher had pressed charges. By then the story had grown. The teacher swore up and down that the whole thing was a plot this fifteen year old girl had, and that through "…underworld connections she was going to have me killed!" The police officer and everyone else thought it was silly, but the old teacher insisted, so they had to set a court date. Mama Jo would have to appear in juvenile court.

Meanwhile, Mama Jo had a little part-time job. She worked for her neighbor across the street, an older woman named Mrs. Smith. Mama Jo also happened to have a crush on this woman's son, a much older man. Mama Jo was a hard worker; she spent a lot of time at the house doing odd cleaning jobs and whatnot. She was also there to serve as an inspiration for Mrs. Smith's granddaughter. Conchita was an only child, rather fragile and terribly underweight. Mama Jo's companionship seemed to help the girl to eat.

Everything took a fateful turn when Mama Jo confided one day in Mrs. Smith about her upcoming court date. The woman filled Mama Jo with fear, saying things like, "You could go into that court, and they could smack you and neither you nor your mother could do anything about it," and "You can't go to court because your mother just doesn't know what can happen!" Who knows why she would fill my mother's head with these things, but she did. Her late husband had been an attorney, so she had some credibility in the eyes of a young girl. When Mrs. Smith told Mama Jo to tell her mother that she wasn't going to court, Mama Jo took it to heart. She could never "tell" her mother any such thing. Now, Mrs. Smith could have offered to talk to her mother, Mrs. Tang, on Mama Jo's behalf, but she didn't. Instead, the day before the court date, Mrs. Smith told Mama Jo to go home and pack a bag, and offered to hide her away until the court date passed. Subsequently, they transferred her to another house, and Mama Jo hid out at the home of Minister Maze and his wife.

Not knowing what to do, my grandmother, Mrs. Tang, went to court, explaining that her daughter was missing. She eventually figured out the connection with Mrs. Smith, but her hands were tied. Someone at the court told her that in order to really take action she would have to file a charge of some sort. Since there was an older man in the mix, I guess the natural inclination was to file a charge of statutory rape. My grandmother wanted her daughter back, so that's exactly what she did. Naturally, the court was sympathetic to Mrs. Tang.

So, the tide had turned, and now Mrs. Smith and her son had a charge of statutory rape to face. The story goes that the two women ended up on the same streetcar on the way to court and never said a word to one another. They sat there in court, my grandmother just waiting to see her daughter and my other grandmother, Mrs. Smith, waiting for her moment. When she was called, Mrs. Smith produced a marriage license with his name and my mother's on it. The charges were dropped. That's how my mother and father came to be married.

Come to find out, my mother had no idea what was going on behind the scenes, including the statutory rape charge. All the while that she was hiding out at the reverend's house, Archie—my father— was calling on her periodically. He would tell her to "dress up real nice" because he was taking her downtown. Well, one time he told her that they would be getting blood work done and a license because they were going to get married. To that fifteen year old girl, it was the ultimate ego-boost. An older man wanted to marry her! To her it meant that he loved her. The next time that Archie called her, it was for a wedding date. They headed down to the Justice of the Peace, and that was that.

That's how life began for my family of Brittons. When all was said and done, Archie took Mama Jo back to his mother's house. They lived there until their second child was born. When I was born, my mother was twenty-three and my father was fifty. Mama Jo stayed with him until he died when I was twelve years old. I remember hearing talk of divorce now and then, of Daddy asking us which parent we kids wanted to live with, but that was just him talking. Mama Jo never indulged such things. In her mind, she had made a vow before God and intended to stand by it, for better or for worse. He would do his best, and she would do hers. In retrospect, I'm sure that they did just that.

Mom—
Interpreter of Dreams

I have always dreamt in color and feel my dreams very powerfully. During the years that my youngest sister, Wee-Bit, was suffering with seizures and I was living in New York, my dreams became even more symbolic and intense. I was thankful for them, actually. I called home and visited all the time, and I had all the more conversations with Mama as she helped me to see the symbolism in those images and scenarios that played out in my brain.

There are a couple of dreams, in particular, that really stand out from that time. In one of them I am staying in this little Victorian house on Alexander Street in Rochester, New York. (There were actually a lot of those houses in that area.) Anyway, these homes typically had a long entry hallway that turned into the dining room and living room. In the dream, I was sitting there on my sofa and this big rat walks into my house. Of course, I'm startled and scared. I yell at it, "Get out of my house!" The rat turns into a cat and walks out, just like that. I woke up with the most disturbing feeling. With all of the dreams I was having at this time, I was usually able to just let them go, but this one just sort of haunted me.

Finally, I called Mama. She said that when you dream of rats, it means you have secret enemies. Now, the first thing that came to mind for me was the fact that I was working for Xerox, in an all-white, male organization. My boss, whom I'll call Bob, was Polish, blonde, over six feet tall, had the corporate look, and worked on the marketing side of the house. I had never interviewed with Bob, but he was the one I reported to. Well, after further discussion with Mama, we realized that none of these guys I worked with were a secret to me.

Finally, she concluded that the fact that the rat transformed into a very compliant, domesticated cat added another layer to the meaning.

The real metaphor in the dream was that I had a friend that I perceived as an enemy on the surface. *Wow!* I thought. That thought shone a different light on my work experience, although I didn't really understand it at the time. I went through a lot of trials at Xerox, partially because I was a bit militant and angry in some of the stands I took. Don't get me wrong; I have no regrets and I really helped to institute some long overdue change in that corporation. It just wasn't easy. The bottom line is that while I did truly have some enemies at the company, Bob did, indeed, turn out to be a supporter. He truly had my back and took a lot of heat for it. So, the dream was about my relationship with my boss… and my friend.

The other stand-out dream is full of beautiful and horrible imagery. In it, I'm standing in this room, surrounded by all kinds of familiar women—sisters, friends, women I know from all different circumstances. My mother is in the center of the room. It sounds like angels are playing music, just light and beautiful sounds. Everyone seems oblivious and joyful.

Suddenly, to my horror, I look down and see that my mother is standing in the largest pool of bright crimson blood that I had ever seen. I'm the only one who sees it; everyone else is carrying on, having a beautiful time. I don't know if it's menstrual blood, but in my hand, I have a rag and I start trying to wipe up the blood. I'm very self-conscious for myself and for my mother, but even she is oblivious. She's just enjoying herself in this gorgeous setting.

Naturally, I had to ask Mama about this dream, too. She said that when you dream of blood, it means you are or will be victorious. So from then on, any time that I'd share my work stories with her and detail of the shenanigans that those guys I worked with were pulling, she would just remind me of my dream and assure me that I would be victorious. All in all, I did end up being victorious by the time I left Xerox. It was a long road, but it ended well.

Still, I was disturbed by this dream. Years later, I did move back to Chicago after leaving Xerox. It would have been late '92 or '93, somewhere in there. Well, Mama and I had some time alone during the day. She was helping to raise my sister's children at the time, and they were at school. My son was at school, in kindergarten. The dream came back around in broad daylight.

The two of us were sitting there at the kitchen table, as we had so very many times. At that point, Mama was having a lot of problems with her diabetes and blood sugar. She was very hungry, so I made her a peanut butter sandwich. Well, she was practically inhaling it; it had her complete focus. Meanwhile, I kept hearing this sound. I kept looking back toward the kitchen sink behind me because I thought I was hearing the drip, drip, drip of water. Then it sounded like there was more water dripping into a puddle. I got up to check the faucet, and lo and behold, I saw it! My mother—completely oblivious—sitting in her chair, surrounded by a puddle of crimson blood. The next thing I knew, I was on the floor, doing exactly what I had done in the dream. Wiping up blood and trying to stop the source. It was absolute déjà vu, a premonition realized, I guess.

The blood was literally shooting out of her leg, coming from one of the leg ulcers that she struggled with due to diabetes. This one ulcer was particularly deep; it was as if the veins had ruptured. She didn't feel a thing, I guess, and had left it open, trying to get it to heal. She definitely was in no pain. I had to quickly tie a rope around her leg to stop the bleeding, bandage it, and take her to the doctor. If I had not been there, she would have bled to death while enjoying a peanut butter sandwich.

So, in a sense, Mama was right about the interpretation of that dream. I was victorious. I brought my time with a major corporation to a satisfactory end and came back home to be with my family. Mama and I were both victorious. We were together and probably saved her life. Maybe my baby sister, Wee-Bit, played a part in that victory, too. After all, she was the one who'd been telling me that I needed to come home.

Technicolor Dreams

I kept my dreams to myself for a long time. When I went away to high school, a lot of things changed for me, most of which are subject for other stories. Significantly, my youngest sister, Wee-Bit, and I started talking about our dreams during those high school years. We shared a lot of the same experiences living away from home. Just as important, though, were the times we shared back at home, sitting up late at night with Mama.

A lot of times, we came home for the weekends. After a long bus or train ride, we'd sit in the kitchen and wait for Mama to come home; she worked the night shift. It seemed like she always brought home Chinese food for us. It was a like we were having a celebratory dinner, and we'd sit up most of the night, just talking, eating, catching up. We always looked forward to those times. They grounded us in the life from which we'd branched out.

I don't remember how or why we started talking about our dreams, but we did. Wee-Bit was afraid to dream. Somehow, she learned how to stop or change her dreams in the process because she said they always came true. Not me. I loved to dream and still do. I can, though, wake myself up if it's a dream I don't like, but I can't intentionally change the course of them. As for Mama, she said she was always too tired, didn't have time to dream. It makes sense; she always had a pretty full plate. My brother didn't care much about dreams, and my older sister simply said, "Dreams? I fall asleep and wake up and everything's just fine!" So, it was mostly Wee-Bit and I.

Wee-Bit dreamt in black and white. I, on the other hand, always dreamt in Technicolor. I had the typical dreams, like falling, but I'd always wake up before I hit the ground. One of my other dreams was much more memorable, partially because it was quite morbid and partially because I had it over and over again. It started when we lived on Lake Street, at the old place before we built the new house. It was sort of an industrial neighborhood, but there were some residences and we still had some friends there: Tonya, Eletha, and Lawanda were a few of them. Well, my sisters and I were always on the go, always playing here or there. I remember countless times running out the front door and past two buildings, through an empty lot on the corner and across the street to Maypole, where those friends lived. They were around the same ages as my sisters and me.

Those girls were being raised by their grandmother. Sometimes my mother wouldn't let us play there, so we had to stay in front of the house. To compensate, we'd go get a board or something from the empty lot and make our own little seesaw. Well, I was in probably second or third grade, and we always had to be back home just before sundown. So, one evening, we heard Mama yelling for us from the kitchen, calling each of us by name. Well, Dimples, my older sister jumped off the seesaw while I was up in the air. As she was yelling, "I'm gonna beat you into the house!" I came crashing down to the ground and cut open my leg on a rusty nail that was in the board. I made it into the house with a trail of blood behind me. I ended up in the local clinic for a very painful tetanus shot and some excruciatingly painful stitches.

As a result, I had this recurring dream. In it, I'm on the seesaw, playing with my sisters, when a man comes out of nowhere. It's getting dark The street lights are coming on. The man snatches one of us (it's weird, but I can't remember which one of us). I'm kind of outside of myself, so I'm not sure what's really going on or to whom it all happens. After he nabs the girl, though, he cuts off her legs so she can't run away, and takes off down the street. I never wanted to believe it was me in that dream, but I know it came from the real-life experience… and it all happened in vivid color, night after night until we moved from that house when I was ten years old. It didn't matter if I had that dream early in the night or toward morning; I always remembered it. I had other dreams, other nightmares, but that one was the most vivid.

I've had other profound dreams. I dreamed many times about my grandfather after he passed away. Then, after my grandmother died in 2002, I had the most beautiful dream about the two of them. In it, my grandfather walked in through my door, and I said, "How can you be here? You know you passed away!" Then my grandmother came in and joined him. They embraced and then started dancing. When I woke up, I knew they were together on the other side.

I guess sometimes your loved ones come to visit in dreams like that. It happened with Wee-Bit, too. I cried for a whole year after she died. It was such a crazy year. At some point, though, I had a dream about my sister that kind of put my mind a little more at ease. In the dream, we're at a small funeral home. I'm behind a curtain with the casket, and people are coming in, taking their seats and mingling. There's a small opening in the curtain, so I can see what was going on.

In the dream, it was my job to look over my sister and make sure that everything was in order before anyone could view her body. It occurred to me that she really looked good, looked like herself, which is unusual. People usually look like some caricature of themselves after the mortician has handled their body. Anyway, in the dream, she gets up and out of the casket. I say, "What are you doing?" She doesn't answer me. She just looks at herself in this big, full-length mirror, making sure that she looks okay. She's as calm as can be, but I'm panicking! I say, "You can't be doing that! Get back in that casket!"

She completely disregards me. She looks herself up and down—obviously quite pleased—and then I get really nervous because she starts to look at her back in the mirror. I'm worried that they might have left her back partially open due to the autopsy or something. Fortunately, I don't see any of that, but I just keep after her to get back in the casket, all the while trying to keep my voice down so that no one suspects that anything unusual is going on.

Finally, she turns and looks back at me with a smile. There, on her forehead over her right eye, is one trickle of bright red blood. I say, "See! You're gonna mess yourself up! You're bleeding! Get back in there!" She calmly wipes away the blood, and it just kind of disappears with her touch. She gets back in the casket and closes her eyes. Then I woke up. My sister had come to visit me to let me know that she was happy, that everything was okay. I felt warm and reassured. She never said a word, but she didn't have to. Her calm, serene manner was all I needed to see to know that she was okay. I remember that dream as clear as day.

The most profound dream of my life, though, was in 1995. It was the most beautiful dream I've ever had. The dream itself was an amazing, almost indescribable blend of music and words. People have always told me to write down my dreams. Well, I never did until I had this one. It's the only dream I've felt absolutely compelled to immediately write down. So I woke up and rushed to grab a pen and paper. I wrote down every word of it and still have it today. It took the form of a poem called "Our Ancestors Rejoice." Now mind you, I've never written a poem in my life, not of my own volition. I swear, though, that I heard a voice saying, "Write this down." I don't remember what the music was like, only that it fit the words perfectly and that it had a very strong, distinct drum beat; if I ever hear it somewhere I will remember it. I do, though, remember trying to write down the words in the cadence in which they were being spoken. I've not edited one word of it; I kept it true to the source.

1/27/95
OUR ANCESTORS REJOICE
A. Y. Britton

Brothers, we know
and understand.
We know your pain
it is ours.

We understand your trials
they also are ours.
When you feel disappointment
we know the feeling.
Even when your efforts are to rise above,
To escape the DESTINY
We know what that is.

When your efforts result in betrayal...degrading us
We know, we know
This we know with bitterness.

When you arrive...achieve SUCCESS
Your success is ours to share. Rejoice!
Although, often bittersweet,
We share this.

For WE have born you
We have shared the same house,
Played the same games
Walked the same path
Seen the same gloomy visions of our journey
Eaten the same food
at the same table.

Experienced the same inhumanities

For a time, we were one,
One in the same.

Your experience is our experience.

Since the time of Our Ancestors

We have withstood the pain
Like surgery without anesthesia
We have felt each excruciating infliction
as the instrument were used to RIP us apart
Destroying the innocent
    Destroying the bonds of our family
        Destroying our God given right, to **BE**.

We have watched the cloak of deception descend upon us
as the angel of manipulation soothed our wounds

Today, we stand
    Wounded
        maimed
            drugged
We stand.
    Isolated
        disappointed
         misled
            Corruptly informed

We stand.

Our Ancestors rejoice,

We withstand.

As the cloak broadens the angel grows weak.
We withstand.

Our Ancestors rejoice.

For they have given us what the angel can't see and doesn't
understand.

Ancestors Rejoice,

We withstand
another day.

I have shown this poem to my mother, my family, and some of my close friends. I try to read it aloud in the original rhythm, though my memory has faded and I'm sure that I don't do it justice. Still, the feeling that it invoked—and that it seems to bring out in those that I share it with—has not faded one bit. It's beautiful. I often think of my son when I think of this dream. When he was very young, he said to me, "What if when we dream, that's when we're really living—that's our real life, and when we think we're awake is when we're really asleep?" I don't claim to know the answers to those kinds of things, but I think that there's a definite time and space when what we call dreams and what we call life overlap and intermingle.

Wee-Bit Gets
Stricken with Seizures

Sometimes junctures in our lives and in the lives of a loved one happen simultaneously but take us down distinctly different paths. So it was with my baby sister and me. In the fall of 1984, I was just beginning my career. I had just completed about ten weeks of field training in Chicago and then headed back to New York. No sooner did I get back there than I got the call from home. No one had details for me. All I knew was that Wee-Bit had had seizures and was in a coma; we didn't know if it was a drug-induced coma for her protection or if it was something out of the doctors' control. What I did know was that I had to get back home… and fast.

Normally that drive from western New York to Chicago took me thirteen hours. After that phone call, my boyfriend Tris and I made it there in nine. I don't remember much of the drive. It was just intermittent stops for gas with the pedal to the metal the rest of the time.

As the story goes, my sister had just gone to pick up a friend of hers. Well, she got a flat tire and called my brother for help. It was right there in the city, so it was easy for her to reach him and easy for him to come to her aid. Thankfully, he got there when he did. As he was jacking up the tire, Wee-Bit went around to the back to get the spare and just simply fell into a seizure, right there on the ground. No one ever saw it coming. I don't know if she went by ambulance or if my brother just loaded her into the car, but he got her to the hospital as soon as possible.

Of course, they had no idea what was causing the seizures when Wee-Bit got to the emergency room. As soon as they would calm her down and she would regain a bit of consciousness, she'd get hit with another one. Grand Mal seizures, that's what they were, and they just kept coming, one right after another. The doctors were perplexed.

They finally had no choice but to put her in a drug-induced coma. Doing so allowed them to monitor her brain. Our question for them was whether she was still seizing with no physical signs of it due to the drugs. The answer was yes.

The brain scans showed that the seizures were coming from somewhere deep in the core of the brain. None of the medications they were giving her were working. The only solution, the doctors said, was surgery. I just remember all of us sitting around this table in a conference room, hearing the words "brain surgery" in reference to my twenty four year old sister. It was just unbelievable, very traumatic. My family and I all prayed about it. Ultimately Mama said, yes, we have to do everything we can for her.

Everything meant brain surgery. The doctors told us that trimming the part of the brain that was triggering the seizures was the only foreseeable possibility. Of course, we were afraid of what the surgery would do to her, too. We didn't want her to come out of it as a vegetable. The doctors assured us that while she would have some memory loss and maybe some motor skill damage, the surgery would not have that kind of adverse effect on her. They would control what they could with medication. So we agreed to that.

The surgery went fine, and she made it through. I remember all of us standing around her when she opened her eyes again for the first time. We were all so excited and talked to her softly. She just stared back at us, looking confused. When we asked her if she remembered anything, she shook her head. I think the first thing she said came when Mama said she had to go to work. Wee-Bit's response was, "What's that?" She didn't know what work was! When we explained Mama's *job* and the *night shift* and all of that, she had no idea what we were talking about. Then we told her that we hoped she could come home for Christmas; it was just a couple of weeks away. Again, her response was, "What's that?" We weren't sure what to say.

The doctors all said how well she came through everything. They closely monitored her for a long time, as they expected to see signs of motor skill damage. But, she could walk and talk and was fully functional. It's funny, but despite all the trauma that she had healed from, there was one nagging little thing that she could just not let go: Her pinky toe on one foot was numb. There was also a big scar on her bald head—she loved to show that off—but the numb toe was a constant source of annoyance. The doctors said, "If that's the only thing that bothers you after brain surgery, you're doing very well!" So that was funny; one thing to smile about looking back.

As far as her brain itself, I think we may never know what she knew and what she pretended to know. The doctors all said that there were some things she could relearn and some memories that were simply gone. Her brain just needed time to heal, plain and simple. She never remembered any of her high school years and had to learn to write all over again. There were a lot of old friends and family members that we had to reintroduce her to. She never remembered our sister Donna and never remembered going to school to be a travel agent. She did remember her one year of college. And she definitely remembered that she loved vodka. I think there were a lot of things that she just kind of went along with. As a grown woman, she surely didn't want us all explaining every little thing to her.

Another thing Wee-Bit remembered was how much she liked to smoke weed. It was pretty ironic because I think that being a reefer-head may have been what caused the whole thing. Now, don't get me wrong; it's purely speculation. She may have had an injury to her brain from the impact of a car accident as a kid, too. But I'll never forget when, early on, the head of neurology, Dr. Barr, was talking with me, trying to figure out where the dark spot on my sister's brain could have come from. She asked me, point blank, where Wee-Bit could have gotten hold of rat poisoning. I would never have revealed my sister's secret to the doctors, but my mind went immediately to the guys she bought weed from. I don't think anyone intentionally poisoned her, but those dealers hung out in the alleys; that was where they stashed their product. And everyone knows that the alleys of Chicago are constantly baited for rats. So I've always wondered if Wee-Bit may have come across some tainted weed. I always used to ask her why she would buy something off of some guy in an alley. If you love to smoke it so much, at least make sure you're getting it from

a solid source! But after the surgery, she was on such high levels of medication to control the seizures that she always looked high, anyway. I always told her to watch herself and not do anything crazy or people would think it was street drugs she was on! We laughed about that. Looking back, we still got to laugh about a lot of crazy things.

Still and all, I know that she longed to have a normal life. Of course, you can't legally drive when you suffer from seizures, but that didn't stop Wee-Bit. Every once in a while, she would steal Mama's car. One time, she had a seizure and wrecked it, wrapping it around a light pole, but somehow managed to walk away from it. Then there were times when she really suffered from depression and threatened to stop taking the medication. She did quit taking it a few times, too, and then fell immediately into the seizures again. She was just trying to lead her own life, but I can't even recount how many times we had to chase her down, only to end up in the emergency room in the aftermath of another accident or seizure or both.

Wee-Bit did manage to live a pretty independent life. After about six months in Mama's care, she moved out and found a place in a building next door. She never worked again but spent a lot of time volunteering at schools and in the community. Luckily for her, she had a cat that was more like a guard dog. Felix watched over her continually. He was funny, loved to eat Ritz Crackers and popcorn and sit at the kitchen table in his own chair across from my sister. When a seizure would come, he would just watch her, defensively hissing at anyone who reached for either her or him. After the seizure would pass, he'd walk back and forth on her back or chest, purring and kneading at her with his paws. He'd be right there resting on her when she woke up again. It was the cutest thing. After Wee-Bit was gone, Mama adopted Felix, but it took some time for him to get used to Wee-Bit's absence.

We worried about her, of course, and did what we could to protect her, but we couldn't exactly strap a crash helmet on her or tie her down. I take that back; my brother did actually tie her down one time! There were several times late at night when she would threaten to go hang out with whomever and she would get really defensive and crazy about it. Well, my brother tackled her in the front yard a number of times. Once, I remember him actually hog-tying her hands and feet and carrying her kicking and screaming back in the house. He wouldn't let her go until she calmed down.

Another time, my sister's determination was like something out of a movie. She was starting to see this guy named Dee, and he was bad news. We all knew it. We also knew that he probably wanted to hang out with her primarily because she looked high all the time. She seemed to attract a certain kind of people to her. Well, he was waiting by the gate for her, but we told her no, she was NOT going to go. She told us otherwise and, after we blocked her from the door, charged for the plate glass window! After bouncing off once, she bolted again and crashed right through it! Somehow, she rolled and bounced back up without a scrape or scratch and off she ran into the night.

There were so many times like that. She had always been stubborn and a bit rebellious, but after the surgery, in many ways she was like a different person. I don't know how she did some of the things she did. She could scale the fence, tuck, roll, and walk away down the street, apparently without a care in the world. After she passed away, we took a close look at a bunch of old photos, taken before and after the surgery. She literally looked like two different people. Some of the changes were subtle, some not so subtle. So, in many ways, we've always felt like we lost Wee-Bit twice.

Ultimately, the doctors were never able to control the seizures. You have to go without seizures for six months to have them considered "under control." That never happened for Wee-Bit. She got sick in '84 and passed away in '92. In all of those years of going back and forth to the doctor, there was never a six-month period when she went without a seizure. They always affect the brain and the heart muscle, but having them that frequently really takes its toll. She knew, of course, that every episode wore on her just that much more. That's probably why she was so bent on living whatever was left of her life to its fullest. Ultimately, her heart did stop during a seizure, and she just never opened her eyes as she lay there.

I think that a good deal of her life was lived at the University of

Illinois Hospital. She had to go there every month for testing. In a way, Dr. Barr, the head neurologist, sort of became her surrogate mom. I really think that her appointments were half testing and gaining information and half complaining about how we wouldn't let her live her own life. It was good, actually, that she had an objective source to go to.

I spent as much time as I could with my sister, going back and forth from New York and my job at Xerox to Chicago and my family. All of my vacation time and many weekends found me back at home. Sometimes, Mama would get so stressed out that she needed a break, too, so I'd get Wee-Bit and bring her back to New York with me for a while. The important thing was, we all supported each other. I think Wee-Bit saw that, and I can only hope that it made her feel more secure. It seemed to me like she really longed for that kind of security and was always on an unspoken mission to get her memory back. As much as she fought us, she also sought out our time and company. She and I took trips together, re-did things we had done before the illness. One of our little adventures took us on a road trip to New York and another to Louisiana.

It was hard to be away from my family at that time. Between Mama and Wee-Bit calling me and me calling them, we were on the phone a lot. It was all very confusing, and I guess I did my best. I'd get conflicting reports, though, with Wee-Bit complaining and griping. Mama was still working the night shift, getting home around midnight or so, and Wee-Bit was trying to help take care of her and watch out for her, too. So, I'd call Mama herself to ask if everything was all right. Of course, she was always one to say that everything was just fine, never one to complain. Finally, after several years of this juggling and balancing act, Wee-Bit kept saying, "It's time for you to come home." Mama would never have said it, but Wee-Bit did. I know that both of them realized I did the best I could.

I felt grateful for those times when we were experiencing them, and even more grateful now. Despite the changes in Wee-Bit, despite the fact that looking into her eyes wasn't like looking into the little sister's eyes that I had known for over twenty years before the illness, I always knew that she was still in there. I saw glimmers and flashes of her in her big, crazy smile. I knew she wouldn't be with us forever, so I took each one of those smiles and stashed it as a memory.

5

THE TERRIBLE SENSATION

The years of Wee-Bit's illness were difficult times for all of us. It seems that I developed my own way of dealing with the stress, the trauma, the sadness, and even the moments of joy and connection with my family. While I had always dreamt in color, my dreams became even more vivid and metaphoric. The bond between Mama and me grew even stronger as, time after time, we spoke on the phone so that she could help me interpret those dreams. I became very intuitive in general. It seemed I always knew when something just wasn't quite right at home. I'd call, and sure enough, something or someone was in need of attention.

The truth and accuracy of my intuitions hit me like a brick wall one morning. I was sitting at work in my cubicle, like any other day. It was bright and sunny outside, but my space was far from the windows, so the natural light had little effect on my portion of the fluorescent-lit room. Out of nowhere, I suddenly felt kind of claustrophobic, like the opposite end of the room had gotten painfully crowded and the space around and above my cubicle had grown dark. I felt very separate from everything and everyone around me. I thought of Mama and Wee-Bit. It was an undeniable feeling that pulled me toward the phone and made me call home.

It was a real relief just to hear Mama's voice. I asked how she was doing, and she responded in her usual manner. So I asked again, explaining this sudden feeling that had come over me. She reassured me that she was fine, and then I asked how my sister was doing. She said she didn't know, that no one had checked on her yet that morning. Mama was raising my older sister's daughters at the time, so she said she would send my young niece to check on her, as she frequently did. I expected to feel better when I hung up the phone, but the feeling didn't subside. It was as if I was a million miles away from my office but somehow stuck there at the same time, mired in something that I couldn't explain.

The phone didn't even get through a complete ring before I picked it up. It was Mama. All she could say to me was, "You need to come home." I'll never forget those words and the impact they carried. Those simple words meant that my sister had died. My poor niece, who couldn't have been more than fifteen years old, had found her and returned to tell her grandmother that her aunt was "cold" and wouldn't wake up.

I had known I needed to go home before I even had a tangible reason to do so. For someone who used to drive back and forth from New York to Chicago in eight or nine hours almost every other weekend, it was unlike me to choose a slow route, but I took the train back home that time. I needed to just be, to sit alone in my compartment, to cry, to remember, and to talk with my sister. She was there with me—I know she was—just like she had come to let me know she had passed.

Maybe all of those intensified dreams and intuitions that I experienced after she became ill served a bigger purpose. Maybe without them I wouldn't have been prepared for the moment that she came to me to say goodbye. Either way, I'm glad that she did, that we were somehow together in that last moment between life and afterlife.

115 ACRES

As much as my dad had always been kind of a mystery to all of us, his family had been even more of an unknown, even to Mama. Well, one thing's certain, when I decide to take on a mission it's underway before I even realize it. So it went with the idea of learning more about my roots.

The opportunity came while I was with Xerox, around 1989. I was working in a training organization at the time, developing an interactive training video. All of the draftsmen working on copier designs were still drawing by hand. It was my job to migrate them all over to computer-based technology. Xerox was using a phenomenal CAD/CAM system where you could draw pictures in a wireframe, and the computer simulation would translate them to 3D or to a solid so you could run a test on it. Well, before I could train others, I had to learn the system myself.

It so happened that the two-week training course would take me to Huntsville, Alabama. My son was three years old at the time, which meant that I would normally have taken the option of flying home on the weekend. It quickly occurred to me, that I had just been presented with the opportunity to seek out some missing limbs of the family tree. We didn't know much more than the fact that Dad had had left the south when he was a small child and had never gone back. His mother had left his father and moved north to Chicago with him and his sister. He never saw his father again. Mama agreed that I should take the time to do some research. The trip was on, at least tentatively.

As I got older, I had learned that Daddy knew he had seven uncles on his father's side, and they were all feuding over the family land that they owned in the Ouachita Parish in Louisiana. It all came down to money and control, of course. There was valuable timber on the land. What's more, there was speculation that there might be oil there, as well.

Long before my father died—when I was still quite young—Tenaco Oil came knocking at our door looking for signatures authorizing them to drill on the land. That was when and how the rest of us found out about the family connection; it became something real and tangible, not just my dad's old distant memory.

I had never ventured into the South before. No one in my family had, either, and I just wasn't sure what to expect. You hear all the stereotypes. Even though it was the late 80s, I proceeded cautiously. I settled into the Residence Inn in Huntsville and found the people to be more pleasant and friendly than I had expected. Some of the locals even directed me to a place that served the best catfish dinner I'd ever had! Feeling more comfortable, I called Mama and told her that I was definitely going on my quest over the weekend. All I had to go on were three names: Ouachita Parish and Amanda and Willis Britton, my paternal great-grandparents.

I planned to leave on Saturday morning for the five-hour drive. But first I wanted to take in some more of the local flavor on Friday night. Now, in Chicago and New York, if you wanted to go out and mingle with other black folks, you went to these very commercial clubs. Not so in Huntsville. One of the local guys, a black guy, who was part of the Intergraph training group, invited us all to party. So that evening, I pulled into this place that must have been an Elks Lodge or something. Very plain and nondescript, no neon sign, no name, no nothing. It was the strangest thing for a woman coming from the big city. It seemed as if these folks had rented a banquet hall with a temporary bar set-up and some music going. But I kind of liked it and started mingling, chatting with people about my trip to Louisiana.

I was preoccupied with the fact that I had to drive through Mississippi. I knew nothing of that state except what I had seen on television and heard on the radio and read in the papers during the Civil Rights Movement and the Martin Luther King marches. All I knew was that they were not friendly to black people. I told myself that all of those things had happened over twenty years ago. How bad could it be now? Well, one of the guys gave me some indirect advice along those lines. He told me to gas up completely in Alabama and drive right through Mississippi. "Don't go over the speed limit, but don't stop 'til you get to Louisiana," he said. He wouldn't explain any more than that, and it put a fear in me.

Given that fear, I carefully plotted my timeline. I decided to leave before dawn to make the five-hour trek. I called Mama and told her that if I didn't find anyone by one or two p.m., I'd turn around and head back to Alabama. God knows I didn't want to get stuck driving through Mississippi at night! I told her what route I'd be taking so that, in case something happened to me, she'd know where to start looking.

I got up the next morning with a lump in my throat and a knot in my gut. Part of me was telling myself that this sounded like some sort of "Roots" experience… and how stupid it seemed. The other part of me was saying that if I didn't do this, no one else would. So, with that thought and Mama's words of support ringing in my head, I grabbed a cup of coffee from the hotel lobby and got in my rental car.

It would be a smooth trip, I told myself, because it was all interstate highway. I did, indeed, stop for a full tank of gas before entering Mississippi, and on the seat next to me was my trusty companion, my map all marked up with my route. Thinking of all the horror stories I had heard of lynchings and what not, I was glad that I didn't have an Afro at the time. I had the permed, corporate-look hairdo. My fears soon gave way to the absolutely beautiful landscape all around me. It was hard to believe that I was driving on an interstate. There were the biggest, tallest, greenest trees I had ever seen on both sides of the highway. Still, I thought, *If you broke down or were stopped along the road, they could be sure you disappeared into the thick woods and were never seen again*! That kept me looking at my speedometer, making sure not to exceed the speed limit. I didn't want any reason to be pulled over. I tried to listen to the radio and stick with my determination.

Crossing through Vicksburg, it wasn't long before I saw the sign saying, "Welcome to Louisiana." Finally, I was able to stop at a visitor center and go the restroom! I had made the drive without stopping once. From that point, it was about another hour before I made it into a city called Monroe, one of the bigger cities in the Ouachita Parish. Plan A was to go to the county courthouse to look up some names and records. As I was driving around, it finally occurred to me that it was Saturday… and the courthouse was closed! It was eleven a.m., and the only official building that I thought might be open was the post office. I don't know what I was thinking! But the post office seemed like a good idea at the time. Turned out the post office was closed, too. Then I had another brilliant idea. I got the phone book and copied down numbers for all of the Brittons; I figured I had a couple of hours to make some calls. Well, as I was coming out, another car parked near mine, and a family got out: a man, woman, and child. Out of pure desperation I asked if they would help me.

"You know," I started, in a shaky voice, "I'm not from around here, but I'm looking for my family. I know I have family down here." I told them my great grandparents' names.

"Hmm…" the woman said, and out of her mouth came my new glimmer of hope as she turned to her husband. "Ain't one of your cousins married to a Britton?" My heart leapt!

He asked what Britton I was looking for. I told him I had no idea. He said, "Well, all the Brittons I know…. the oldest ones live out in Calhoun, Louisiana. They all go to Jerusalem Baptist Church. I betcha a dollar to a dime you're gonna be in that church tomorrow morning!"

I was thinking to myself, *Sir, if I don't find somebody in the next two hours, I'm gonna be back safe and sound in a hotel in Hunstville tomorrow morning!* Of course, I didn't say that. I just politely asked him for directions to Calhoun. I hadn't eaten yet, so I decided to give myself some time to collect my thoughts and make a plan. Over my lunch I decided I had two options and two hours to make the most progress I could. I could passively make phone calls or I could get in the car and go meet some people in Calhoun. I got in my car and headed back to the interstate.

I followed the very precise directions the man had given me. I saw the sign that said Calhoun. When I next turned at the blinking light and into the gas station, as directed, I swear I entered the Twilight Zone. The place was just a different time and place to me. The gas pumps had round glass tops, looked like they were thirty or forty years old or something (just like in the Twilight Zone). Then this black man came out. All he had on was overalls. Now, I hadn't seen overalls—period—since I was a kid on the farm in Indiana, let alone on a black man with no shirt underneath with only one side hooked and the other one hanging down. I'd only seen that kind of clothes on white Mennonite and Amish farmers! I forced myself out of the car to ask for directions.

From this man's mouth I heard a wonderfully slow, southern drawl, the kind of thing I'd only heard in movies. He gave me very elaborate and colorful directions, including phrases like "fork in the road." I had no idea what he meant at first. We just don't use terms like that up north. All of this added to the "Twilight Zone" experience. Intersection, right turn, left turn… yes. Fork in the road, no. Then he just stopped and gave me a puzzled look. "Well, who you lookin' for cuz ain't nobody at Jerusalem Church today. It's Saturday. Ain't nobody gonna be there!"

I told him I actually had no idea who I was looking for and went into my whole spiel again.

"Hmm…" he said, rubbing his chin. "Well, you know what? Floyd, yep Floyd, Floyd Britton will know who you belong to. You need to go to Floyd Britton's house. It's easier to find, anyway." So he gave me directions. Fork in the road, past the schoolhouse, one more house, house on the hill with a trailer, very next place is a farm. "That's where Floyd Britton is."

I asked for a phone number. "Shouldn't I call first?" I asked

"Nah, nah, just go on down there. Floyd's home, he'll know who you belong to."

I thanked him and got back in my car. Again, I had these conflicting thoughts in my head as to whether I should proceed or just turn around and get the heck back to Huntsville. It was noon already, and I hadn't even called Mama to let her know where I was. I came to where the road split in two directions and decided that this must be the "fork in the road," although any fork I had ever seen had at least three or four prongs. I arrived at what must be Floyd's house and realized that I was firmly on the back roads when I had assured Mama and myself that I would stay on the interstate!

Well, I got out and pressed on. It was a nice little brick house, a little unkempt, but what you'd expect of a farmhouse. I realized that to reach the only door I could see, I would have to go through the garage. I was on someone's private property without even having made a phone call first! I made my way to the door. I knocked and called hello. To my surprise I heard, "Yeah, come on in." Tears welled up in my eyes.

I hesitated, of course, and said, "Hello? I'm looking for Floyd Britton." I heard a man saying he'd be just a minute and then saw him coming to the door, fastening up his overalls, with no shirt, just like the man at the gas station. Now, a strange man getting dressed as approached me in the middle of nowhere just about shot my nerves! At this point, tears were starting to slowly flow down my cheeks.

Well, he stood there looking at me through the screen door. "Yeah, I'm Floyd. Who you looking for?" He paused and looked at me more closely. "Sherry?" I told him no. "Well, who are you then?"

I guess I didn't really answer him. I just told him my story, and he kept saying, "Well, you look like so-and-so. Are you her?"

I finally got to the part about my great grandparents' names. His eyes flew open, and he said, "That's my grandparents! Come on in!" while pushing open the screen door. Tears were streaming down my face, and they weren't tears of joy. I was just plain scared, alone in the backwoods with this stranger who now seemed to be related to me. I didn't know what to think! I was violating every instinct of self-protection I had.

The next thing I knew I was sitting at the kitchen table talking with this man. I told him how the man at the gas station had directed me to him. "Well, you've come to the right place!" he said. Then the conversation got very confusing for me. He was asking me all kinds of questions while I tried to explain very clearly where I had come from and what little I knew about my father's family. In the middle of it all and through my tears, I asked to use the phone to call my mother. I was sure I was getting everything all mixed up, so I asked him if he would like to speak to my mother.

Well, it seemed that Mama was able to put the pieces together a little more easily. She explained how my father and his sister Ernestine had ended up going north with their mother. I kept hearing Floyd say, "Oh!" and "Yeah!" and knew they were making connections. Finally, I heard him give my mother his phone number, which put my mind at ease, and I stopped crying. I took a deep breath and let the realization settle on me that I was finally sitting in the house of a relative.

I got to talk to Mama briefly. After we hung up, it wasn't two minutes later that the phone rang. It was my Aunt Ernestine calling, and she was able to give Floyd some more information. It must have all come together for him because that's when he said, "Oh my goodness, Uncle Arthur!" about my dad's dad. He was so excited and happy to talk. As soon as he hung up, he dialed five numbers (again like in the Twilight Zone). "Dorothy," he said, "you won't believe who's sitting in my kitchen!" Floyd had only heard stories about his Uncle Arthur, my grandfather, and that he had moved up north and had children somewhere. "You got to see Dorothy," he told me.

Dorothy was his baby sister, a young black woman with a lovely home. Arriving there, I was really starting to feel at ease. She and Floyd kept naming family members whom I apparently resembled. She, in turn, was so excited, too, and called another sister, Katherine, in Washington D.C. The two of them were going on and on about how this thing was turning into our own "Roots story" and how *exciting* this was, the exact opposite of my thoughts earlier on.

Well, the next thing I knew, I was surrounded by my father's long-lost family. Long story short, it turned out that Floyd and his siblings were actually my father's first cousins. His brother, another Arthur Britton, showed up, as did his daughter, Bean, and his wife, Laura. It really was getting too late for me to drive back, so I stayed at Floyd's house. I was far from prepared to stay, but the next morning found me at the Jerusalem Baptist Church in the same clothes I had worn the day before. I swear, everyone I met there was related to me in one way or another! Some were mulatto and some were dark skinned. I was just amazed. Time and again people shook my hand and said,

"Hi. I want to introduce myself. I am so-and-so, and we must be cousins because my uncle is Uncle Arthur…" and so on.

There were Brittons or relations of Brittons everywhere. The church happened to be on Britton Road, and down that road from the church was a graveyard, called Mount Jerusalem, filled with headstones of Brittons. So I got taken on a tour of the surrounding area. It turns out that the land that our immediate family is part heir to belonged to our great-grandmother, Amanda Britton. It's 115 acres of beautiful wooded land. There are actually more than one hundred descendants who are heirs to that land that no one has lived on since Amanda died back in the early 1900s. The house was no longer standing. You could tell where it had been, though, because it was all overgrown with purple crocuses. The most outstanding thing about the area surrounding the home site was this tree, this amazing tree. You could have hidden a car behind it. The trunk was literally wider than a car. I smiled when I saw it because it occurred to me that we would need a tree that sturdy and that large to hold all of the branches of this family that I had just discovered.

5

Xerox and the Round Table

There truly is power in numbers. I saw it as a child when the Mennonites came together to help us complete our home. I saw it in high school with the formation of the Black Awareness Group. As my time with Xerox was winding down—before I was, indeed, on my way out—I experienced it again.

One day in 1990, I was copied on a letter out of the clear blue. It was a communication to all of the black women in the technical side of the Design and Manufacturing organization, asking if we had issues concerning our promotion—or lack thereof—and attrition. There were maybe a dozen names on this letter, and for a week or so, no one responded. I actually tried to set aside, too, but just couldn't get it out of my head.

One of the names on that list was that of my friend Jocelyn. She was also a Chicago native and a graduate of DeVry. Finally, I called her up. "Jocelyn, did you get this memo from Human Resources?" Well, she said she had, of course, but that she had no intention of responding. Like probably every one else, she just didn't see the point. She figured it was just paying lip service to an obvious problem that the company never really intended to address. Part of me agreed with her, but part of me felt that familiar stir that just told me I had to take action of some sort. I turned to the only person that I thought might be able to give me some sound advice. I called her my mentor, who had left Xerox two years earlier to start her own company. Well, she said, "Yes! Absolutely!" when I asked her if she thought we should do something. I was off and running.

I guess the momentum I had just from that phone call was infectious because Jocelyn got on board after that, too. She had a great idea. She said that we should use the tools Xerox had already given us to address the problem. In other words, we had all gone through problem solving/management training/ etc. using specific, objective techniques. Ironically, we decided to use them to solve an issue that was directly affecting us in the company. Funny how things turn around like that sometimes. We would address our issue in typical Xerox fashion!

We started calling up all of the other women who had received the memo. At the time, I lived in a nice little suburb called Brighton, right outside of Rochester. I volunteered to host the meetings. We met a few Sundays in a row for a couple of hours, and it worked brilliantly. We employed the five-step process that we borrowed, quite conveniently, from our employer. Essentially, we just engaged in non-judgmental brainstorming to identify the problem. Then we came up with a problem statement. We refined that statement until everyone was in agreement on it. We then brainstormed on possible solutions. We stated the top five solutions and an appropriate timetable in which the company could address them. The end result was a brilliant response to the original letter from HR. It didn't apply to anyone in marketing or sales. It was just we women on the technical side of the house.

Promotions had come quickly early on at Xerox. That is, we engineers all came into the company at a Grade 6, which was Project Engineer. We pretty easily made it to Grades 7 and 8, which meant we were Senior Project Engineers. Everything halted, though, when it got to Grade 10, which meant a jump to management. Few of us were breaking through that glass ceiling and getting to Grade 10, which would have meant being a bona fide manager with an actual office and a door, not just a cubicle. Jocelyn, others, and I had been with the company for six or seven years at that point, and we were simply stuck. I had had this nagging feeling for a long time. Even my performance reviews possessed this subtle, vague language—like a secret code—that unsettled me. On the surface, my reviews were good, but not good enough to get me over the hump.

The timing was great. There was an upcoming annual conference of the black employees, and the president of the corporation was going to address this meeting of 3000 or 4000 people. Now, technical people didn't always participate in this event, but we felt it was important to

get tied into it, and we had the support for our concerns from a lot of people in other departments. While none of us could be sure who had gotten the ball rolling with this issue in the first place, rumor had it that the original push had come from the president's young black intern. People seemed to believe that she had put a bug in his ear about what she saw as the disparity in promotions between black women and other employees.

Regardless, it was our time to be heard. The challenge was in getting one simple question into the ear of the company's president and put him to task. So we set up a sort of task force in our hotel room the night before he was to speak and take questions. All of us women put our heads together again, including my mentor, Bernie, who was kind enough to show up. While I had the final hand in getting it down in writing, I was more than happy to hand it off. The problem was, there were no takers! Once again, the responsibility was mine, so I took it. I asked just one thing… that everyone write reminders in colored pen all over this sheet of paper: *breathe, slow down, relax!* When I got the president's attention, I felt so wobbly that I was sure everyone in the room could see how nervous I was, but I pulled it off. The question went something like this:

"We technical black females have been recruited to Xerox from all across the nation and from some of the best technical programs. We have come from programs that Xerox specifically designed, such as the Engineering Development program. The intention of this program was to give us a well-rounded experience to better qualify us to design marketable products and devices. Xerox has invested all this time in allowing us to have this experience with the promise and intention that this company would allow us to move up the ranks of the corporation, and yet we have found that we are unable to be promoted. So, Mr. President, what is your commitment to your technical black females in your organization with regards to promotion?"

It was a very direct question to ask the head of a major corporation. It got his attention and worked its way back around to human resources. One of the main points that came out of the subsequent discussions was that we black women didn't have mentors, people who were pushing us and coaching us along in the company. Managers had assumed that we did but weren't promoting us because they also assumed our mentors would. The upshot of all of it was that we were each assigned a mentor; the VP of Human Resources became mine. The mentors all had us start interviewing for in-house positions in order to force the issue of moving us up the corporate ladder.

It was a long time coming. As a result, I had been given an "*opportunity!*" A *lateral* move as a Customer Acceptance Test Manager. My boss in that position was named Bob. He had grown up on the marketing side of the company, but we had been with Xerox the same amount of time. Well, he was a Grade 12 or 13 manager. I was still a Grade 8, despite the fact that my new "opportunity" was a Grade 10-12 role. I had to take the position, but I was fighting mad and didn't mind letting it show. Bob was a little stunned because I didn't pull any punches with him. In a conversation we had shortly after I took the job I said point blank, "We've been here about the same amount of time, but you're a Grade 12, and I'm an 8. Do you really think you're that much smarter than I am?" He couldn't even respond.

Our original letter had stipulated a timeline of one year. I felt like we had come a long way since then, at least in our principles, if not in results. We wanted all of our goals met within that time, including having a black female vice president on the engineering side of the house. Despite our lofty goals, we were also realistic. We women had very frank discussions among ourselves acknowledging the fact that Xerox most likely would not implement all our solutions. We knew we had set things in motion but that it would be future black female employees who would reap the benefits. Our backup plan was simple attrition, a mass exodus that would get even more attention.

That's exactly what happened. People were promoted to 9s and 10s. Then all progress stopped. Now, Rochester is a cold place. No one was too upset about the idea of leaving, of looking for more rewarding work in a nicer locale. Within a year, only a handful of the women involved in our big push remained with the company. The rest of us left. Ironically, the company was paying for some of us to

get MBAs… and then not providing the challenging and rewarding positions to go with the degree. So these women said, "Thanks for the education. Here's my resignation," and went on their merry ways.

As for me, I put in for a transfer to Chicago. It was a difficult time. My sister Wee-Bit's illness was getting worse, taking its toll on everyone. Mama wanted me to come home. It came down to a numbers game, really. The corporation needed to show that it was an Equal Opportunity Employer on both sides of the house, so they simply needed me where I was, in Rochester, in engineering. I put in for numerous positions beyond engineering and haggled time and again with HR.

I never got that transfer, and it wasn't long after that that I left the company. Looking back, I know that we left some positive change in our wake. On a personal level, I'm so glad that I felt compelled to respond to that original letter from HR. I set people in motion, once again, toward a positive goal. I've been in situations where I'm the only one, the first one ever, or part of a very small crew. In '84, there weren't that many black engineers period, let alone black female engineers. We really were a rare breed of women at that time. And so it seems I've always found myself in situations where I am the voice or lead the way for others to find their own voices. If that's a gift that I can give, then I'm happy to be the bearer of it. I have to think back to my high school experience. Those first two years on the farm kind of set me up to become that person, outspoken and analytical. I became the person that the voice inside of me wanted me to be.

Crabs in a Barrel—
The Birth of
Five Black Women

They say when one door closes another opens. Looking back at the time when I was preparing to leave Xerox, I can see that another door was, indeed, opening for me. I've been taking small steps toward that threshold ever since!

It helps to have a mentor as you move toward any change. For me, that person was Bernie Poole. With a PhD from Columbia University, she came in through Corporate Headquarters on the marketing side but ended up on the technical side because the company needed black women over there. She was about twenty years older than me, and with all of her wisdom and experience, she actually became a mentor for a lot of us black women. We were all in the same predicament, almost like crabs in a barrel, all trying to climb up, inadvertently stepping all over each other even when there was nothing to climb to. Little did I know at the time that eventually we would get the letter from HR and form the Black Women's Round Table. She was ahead of all of us. She had bigger ideas, bigger plans.

Bernie and I became very close and spent a lot of time together. I had gone through a difficult divorce, and she even became my son's godmother. Over glasses of wine on the weekends we spent a lot of time talking about our futures. She wanted to start her own company, become an independent consultant. After all of the frustrations we had experienced over lack of promotions at Xerox, we talked a lot about experiences of professional black women. Her idea was to form a technical training organization called Aedutech. So, at its core, the concept of Five Black Women spawned from Bernie's desire to leave Xerox and start her own company. And she did. Her company still exists today.

Time and again we came around to one consistent idea: If we could take just five of these black women at Xerox, we could start our own corporation. We would have a Board of Directors comprised of educated black women: MBAs, PhDs, engineers. Five Black Women… It would make the perfect acronym, I thought. FBW. Like IBM. No one else needed to know what FBW stood for! It was a brilliant idea, an ideal. Hence, Five Black Women was conceived. In the meantime, though, we were trying to keep up with making a living.

Bernie found that, as a black woman, she had a hard time attracting big corporate clients. Years later, after I finally left Xerox, I found the same thing, and it didn't matter what my credentials were. So I decided to go where I was welcome and aimed for the consumer level. First, I decided to get everybody in my family up to speed technologically. They were a safe place to start! I was in this strange dichotomy. It was the early 90s, and I was working with all of these high-tech systems and then coming home to a family where no one even had computers.

Moving back to Chicago meant a big shift for me, not just in lifestyle, but also in my vision for Five Black Women. I went from a corporate focus to a community focus. I looked all around me and saw unmet needs in the inner city, in my community, in my neighborhood. A majority of services—simple things like Laundromats—had left the area long ago. In Rochester I had been used to walking down the street for a gelato, but back home it wasn't safe to walk the block! Now, more than fifteen years later the area is slowly becoming re-gentrified, but it's a slow and painful process.

I went back to my old Mennonite church and was encouraged by a couple of women I had known before. One had become a dentist and one had become a mortician. Both of them aspired to open their own businesses but chose to stay in Chicago and hopefully help their community. That spurred another thought in me: Church is the one institution that gives a lot of strength to and holds together our community. It occurred to me that if I were to attach FBW to a church, our services would have great credibility as a foundation of people truly interested in helping its community. We'd also have a market of people in need.

Our church already had a steady business in its daycare. I brainstormed with some of the church members and came up with a list of about twelve reasonable businesses—including the dentist's office and the proposed mortuary—that could be part of our network. The core of the idea was this: You have people who start a business that they love. Maybe they don't have the technical skills or business savvy to keep it afloat, but they have passion. FBW would serve as the management at the heart of all of these businesses. From there we could form different business units as things grew. That model works because different units experience profit and loss at different times. So, even when a business experiences a drought in the short term, it can survive and thrive in the long term due to being part of this network. Of course, with being attached to the church, part of the profits would go to the church to help it grow and continue its community outreach services, too.

I knew I needed to get my plan in writing, and I did. I developed the plan in conjunction with Bernie and her company, Aedutech. It is called the Strategic Economic Development Plan, and it's dated June 1, 1994. It was originally addressed to the Mennonite Economic Development Association, or MEDA, which has a history of investing in small businesses in economically depressed areas. One of my stipulations was that MEDA recognize the need for a liaison, which could offer a non-white perspective on existing, new, and proposed small businesses. And there needed to be a cooperative strategy that incorporated the Christian mission, the needs of the existing church in those economically depressed areas, and the needs of the small business owner or entrepreneur.

In considering the church at the core of the business model, I realized that I also had to look at the history of the church. Our church was originally subsidized by the larger Mennonite Church in order to extend its ministry into the poor, inner-city neighborhood. There were inherent possibilities for growth within the church and the community: education, employment, youth activities, and senior programs would all grow under the auspices of the church. All of these supports would help members to gain stable employment. However, there are

no decent jobs and limited resources in the local community. So, as people improve their lives, they leave the community that actually helped get them on their feet. That's the Catch-22 and the reason why not every entrepreneur wants to set up shop in a depressed area. My cautionary word was not to try to impose a greater vision on those who were not willing or able to grasp it.

So, here was my overview: Establish a collective, a group of ten small businesses and/or potential business owners. Provide financial, legal, and strategic planning, as well as managerial and educational resources, and apply them to this community. Establish that a portion of the profits benefit the church, which provides the entire foundation. Establish an association based on annual membership. Ideally, the businesses would operate in a sort of co-op where they could be housed in one building with a central business office that grows in support services as the businesses themselves grow. That was the brainchild. I started by working in corporate America and ended up taking my dream into the inner city.

The original group of businesses looked like this: a central office, a literary magazine or the like, some sort of cultural preservation office, some sort of specialized skills training office, a daycare, a preventative/alternative medicine office, an insurance office, a children's book store, an automotive repair center, an off-site bed and breakfast, and an array of others.

Long story short, MEDA did not fund it. Part of the issue of economic development is the fact that it takes more than just seed money to get a business up and keep it running. A lone business popping up in a depressed area is probably going to fail because people simple don't *do* business in a depressed area. As a rule, they commute to the more affluent areas. And a lone business owner knows that they are more likely to be robbed or vandalized than generate sufficient business. They know that for every one person who comes in to actually buy something, several more are going to come in to shoplift.

The idea of the a dozen or so businesses coming in together and taking up a city block or one entire large building makes so much more sense. There's security and power in numbers! By default, people will come to use one business and end up patronizing others. Maybe it was too big of an idea for the early 90s.

Now, almost fifteen years later, this thing has reawakened in me. I look at my original document, and it's as fresh as ever. After all, if you go to the poor, inner city communities, who do you find there? You find the same kinds of people as in the 90s, and even more single mothers than ever before. These women have a smaller chance of leaving than just about anyone. It's a sad fact that so frequently the bedrock of these communities is elderly people and single parents.

Having said that, I would also say that the concept of Five Black Women duplicated over and over again in these communities would have the most profound impact on them. The people in these communities know what they need, where they want to shop, and what kinds of stores would benefit them and their children. What's ironic is that the dollar is the same in affluent communities and poor communities, but the quality of the products is not. There is dog food in stores in my old Chicago neighborhood that I wouldn't feed to my pet.

Like I've said, my mother always asked me where I got my big ideas. She asked me that question when I moved back to Chicago with FBW on my mind, too. From my perspective all of these years later, I would say that I get my big ideas from the sum of my life's experiences… and from the neighborhood that was such a big part of it all. And that's exactly where those ideas need to take root and start growing again!

5

VOLUNTARY REDUCTION AND BACK OFF, BUZZARD!

The Black Women's Round Table had set things in motion at Xerox. There was no turning back for me. When we didn't get what we had stipulated in our original letter, and I didn't get my transfer, I knew that it was time to leave. People kept asking me what I was going to do. I wasn't sure, but I did know that every once in a while Xerox instituted a voluntary reduction in force. I decided I would be one of the first to step up when the time came around.

The reduction was usually intended for the retiring or near retirement age employees. It was basically unheard of at our levels, and managers did not condone it. No one believed I was actually going to go through with it. Essentially, taking the reduction would mean that at my level I would have six months of salary continuance and full benefits. And, the best part… I got to walk away. I thought, *I can do whatever I want, go wherever I want. If I can't figure out my life in six months, then shame on me!*

I signed the paper. Within a day or two, the phone started ringing. Then and there, I was offered the promotion, basically anything I wanted, except the transfer to Chicago. Someone even came to my home in an effort to get me to change my mind. By then, though, it was a done deal. I knew I was going home, and that was that. I started at Xerox in 1984, left in December of '92, and collected my last paycheck in mid '93.

I had one last hurrah before I left. My big boss was named Joe. He was a real SOB, and I wasn't the only one who felt that way. He had never promoted anyone of color and seemed disgustingly proud of that fact. Well, while I was out Christmas shopping for my young son, I saw the perfect gift for the man. I had never bought him a gift before and doubt that anyone else ever had either, except maybe his

secretary out of sheer obligation. But I figured it would be a nice part-
ing gesture on my part—you know, a way to tell him the things I had
always felt without having to say a word. It came in a nice big box. I
wrapped it up beautifully and carried that massive gift into the office.

"It's a present for Joe," I said, beaming, when all of the secretaries
asked whom it was for. I proudly handed it to his personal secretary,
who looked pretty puzzled. I saw her go in and set it on his desk. I
never saw Joe after that. I left and never looked back. I heard that six
months later, he left the company, too. Good riddance. I do wish,
though, that I could have seen his face when he opened my gift. It
was a board game with the name in big letters all across the front:
BACK OFF, BUZZARD! I guess he got the message.

5

Africa

I had always wanted to go to Africa. By 1994, I had left Xerox, my sister had died, and my business proposal had not even been considered for funding. Life was very transitional for me, which meant that it was the perfect time to take my son on a great adventure. Amid questions from everyone about whether or not my son was too young for such a trip, just how the heck I was going to afford it in the first place, and "How can you just go off like that to some foreign land?" I booked us on a tour and off we went, just Khalif and I.

It was kind of a whirlwind; everything was so new to me. The days passed as if I were looking through a camera lens out of the side window of a moving bus. Khalif was so good, though, so patient, just taking it all in, too. We weren't alone on that trip, either, and I don't mean just the other members of the black tour group we went with. My sister Wee-Bit was with us in spirit. You see, she had always been kind of a practical joker. One night, my son and I were at this gorgeous resort—we really stayed in some first class places—and in this particular one, the room was like a loft, with the beds upstairs. We had gotten in late, so I put my son directly to bed and went downstairs for something. When I turned on the water, I couldn't turn it off! It would not stop running. So, there I was in a strange place, a foreign country, in the middle of the night with the downstairs rapidly flooding. It was even running out like a waterfall down the little step at the front entrance. When I ran outside and looked back at that image, I just knew that Wee-Bit was looking at me and laughing. "Gotcha," she was saying. I knew that my son and I were in safe, loving hands.

Naturally, the sun and heat were intense while we there. Luckily I had brought these two beautiful, huge scarves. They were done in a gorgeous, exotic design, as if they should be worn by an Indian princess. I was dating a blues musician at the time, and a friend of his had brought them back from Bali. He'd given them to me as a gift. They came in handy, as we spent a lot of time walking to and from the bus and through the villages. I could wrap my head with them, or several of us could hold the corners and supply shade for five or six of us at once!

I think that those scarves may have brought me good luck in more than just shade. One time, I dozed off on the bus. When I awoke, there was Blaze, one of our tour guides, wrapping one of my scarves around his head and his face like an Arab. Now, Blaze was Muslim and spent a lot of time in prayer, and there seemed to be something so intentional, so almost ceremonial in the way he was wrapping and then unwrapping and then re-wrapping the scarf in the opposite direction. I told him I figured that he was either blessing me or cursing me, and I hoped for the former! He didn't answer; he just looked at me and continued and later made a joke of it. But, with the amazing things that happened the next year, I've often wondered if he did, indeed, offer a blessing.

Another thing that struck me oddly was the whole bartering system. Granted, we were part of a tour group and most of the people I was traveling with were definitely there to shop. One guy even had an African store back in Baltimore. But it just didn't sit right with me that we came from an affluent country to a very poor one and were still trying to drive down the prices we paid! We were literally paying these people pennies for their artwork and crafts.

Well, Sylvester, our other tour guide, had to come to the rescue for me. I literally started arguing with some of the vendors and people in my group. The vendors would yell, "Sister! Sister!" while hounding me to buy the smallest thing. I would yell back, "No, no! I don't want it!" It didn't make sense to me, but Sylvester explained that the bartering is simply part of the cultural exchange.

I finally gave the guy who owned the African shop in Baltimore my money and asked him to shop for me. I ended up with one souvenir, in particular. Another woman bartered down from sixty U.S. dollars to about thirty, and I came home with a wooden carving of a little man squatting. It sat on the floor at Mama's house for a while until the dog was just about ready to have a nervous breakdown, con-

stantly barking and yelping at the thing as if it were taunting and threatening him. Today, it sits in the entryway of my home in Phoenix.

There were some interesting people in our group, too. This one young couple was very into the "Pan-African" thing. They even arranged to get married at a Muslim mosque, even though they weren't Muslim, while we were there. Well, one day we took a trip in Jeeps way back along these trails to a little resort just outside of Dakar. Khalif was fascinated by it. There was a gorgeous pool, a restaurant, and a wild monkey on a chain, from which Sylvester did a good job of keeping Khalif and the other kids at a safe distance. The people who owned the establishment and were hosting it were white, and the young woman (from the couple) announced that she was not going to eat there because she refused to support any kind of white enterprise in the Mother Land; she had come to visit *Africa*! She was just outraged and starting to make a scene, putting a damper on the experience for everyone. Now, this was still in my drinking and smoking days, and I had had a couple of drinks. I asked her if she really thought that the bus company and every resort we had stayed in up to that point had been owned solely by blacks. The thought caught her by surprise, I could tell. I mean, admittedly, you get off the plane and just about everybody you see is black. Unless you do your research, like I had done, and/or really stop to think about it, you don't realize who and what is going on behind the scenes. She even started harassing me about being a Christian, the "white man's religion," while I had a drink and a cigarette in my hands. I simply told her, "I said I'm saved, not perfect!" So then she turned to Sylvester, thinking she'd get this black brother on her side. I cut her off and said, "Well, he's Catholic." That took the wind out of her sails altogether! The girl sort of mellowed out her stance from then on.

My son did a lot of growing up on that trip, too. In fact, he sort of became a little man, protective of his mother. Naturally, there were single men on that trip. Whenever I tried to speak to Blaze or Sylvester, Khalif would kind of wedge his way in and position himself between us. At the Novotel Hotel in Dakar, the whole group was splashing and playing in the pool. Well, there was an older man who was traveling with his daughter and grandchildren. When he playfully told me he was going to dunk me, Khalif—who couldn't yet swim—clung to the side of the pool and pulled himself along hand over hand to the deep end, telling the man, "You're not gonna dunk my mama!" It was quite a sight. And so it went. My boy began to grow up.

It was a good experience, though. I hadn't really realized until this trip that Africa was colonized and that it wasn't until the Civil Rights Movement here that the countries started seeking independence from those who had colonized them. It's so easy to default to thinking that Africans were taken from their country and enslaved in America, but the truth is that Africans were enslaved—or subjected to indentured servitude—in their homeland, too. The Portuguese, French, Germans, and British, etc. had all come in.

Again, I had done my share of study and preparation for this trip. One of the things I knew I wanted to experience while there was a tea ceremony. None of my fellow tourists knew what that was, but Blaze was kind enough to go out of his way to make sure that one sunny afternoon in Senegal we experienced it for ourselves. He told me that if anyone invites you to tea you must graciously accept because it's such an honor. No other tourist had ever asked him about it before, he said, nor had the tour guides ever gotten to work with an all-black group. He told me that he and Sylvester were honored.

The ceremony is not unlike the siesta tradition in Mexico. It happens in the heat of the afternoon. The first brew of tea starts off very bitter. The second is less bitter and so on. It's a metaphor for life, very spiritual. The final tea that you drink is very sweet… like life can be after the bitter lessons. It takes a long time to prepare each round of tea because everyone sits around an open flame where it is brewing. I had one of the best times of my life that day, just feeling so open to the experience and its meanings.

I had another great experience in Senegal, too, during a sort of exchange program where we got to spend time with individual families. Well, Khalif and I joined a Muslim family for a day. In Senegal, at least, the Muslim men can have up to four wives as long as they can support them and the children. So there was this household full of women and children, and we all spoke through a male interpreter. It was hard to ask very bold and candid questions because the women are not supposed to speak in that manner at all, especially in front of men. They kept asking me about my "sticks," about how many I had. Sticks is the term for children. All of the women pitied me for having only one stick. They said that I should come back because they wanted to find me a husband so that I could have more sticks. That was such an interesting concept to me. While I had no desire to have more children as those women did, I utterly respected their joy and their acceptance of me.

One of the things that I found most inspiring is that beyond the growing up Khalif did as a little man, he really came into his own in other ways. My boy found his rhythm in Africa. We went to this one ceremony where the men were playing drums. They allowed Khalif and the other kids on the tour to come up and play music with them. At first, Khalif was completely lost. But when the drummer came over and helped him find the beat, he took hold of it and has never lost it. Now when we listen to music together, he not only hears the bass, he feels it, and you can see it move through him. It's very special to me that it was our trip together that gave him that gift. He also discovered the meaning of his name. His father and I were divorced by the time he was a little over a year old, so there are many things he didn't experience from his dad, who had actually picked out his name. In a gift shop in Senegal, my son noticed the pictures of Khalifas hanging on the wall. In Senegalese, a Khalifa is a spiritual leader. In Muslim and Arabic, it means a successor to the leader. Either way, it's a strong reference, one that made Khalif feel proud.

I experienced more than I ever bargained for, though not every bit of custom and culture was positive and uplifting. Apparently, the people of Mauritania are more caramel colored, like Khalif. To my horror, someone assumed that my son was Mauritanian and explained that there were still slaves there. It had just never occurred to me that people, especially women and children, were still used as commodities in labor and arranged marriages and business deals. Regardless, it was just so interesting to see people of different shades of brown and black

100

in one place. In Morocco, people are more Arabic, and Khalif blended right in there. I, on the other hand, blended in more in Senegal, where people are darker skinned. It was such a new experience to look around me for the first time in my life and see so many people who looked like I did. I've never felt anything like that before. No one had to say a word for me to feel a kinship.

Since we were a uniquely all-black tour group for Sylvester and Blaze, they wanted to share something very special with us. From Dakar, they took us to Gory Island, a small island that was the center of the slave trade for Senegal. I think it had been built by the Portuguese but was taken over by the French. Anyway, once we arrived there by ferry, we were supposed to stick together, move quickly through the crowd and converge as a group at the museum. Groups of black people are ushered in separately from tourists of other races to honor their experience. It was truly a unique and strange experience to be in this enclave with artifacts and pictures of people being herded into holding areas and hung around their chests for being defiant or rowdy—a slow and painful death; describing what had occurred here so long ago.

Other rival tribes would raid villages and bring back men and women; they got top dollar for the strongest men and the most beautiful women. Then the men and women were chained and placed in these virtual dungeons until there were enough of them to fill a ship. From there, they were prodded through what they called the "doorway-of-no-return" to the ship or ships and taken away forever. All the while, interpreters narrated this experience in different languages. The most poignant thing was that it didn't matter what languages were being spoken. The emotion coming through in the words was the same. Like me, I think that almost everyone had tears streaming down their faces—or at least watery eyes—the entire time. I'm glad that my son got to experience that place with me. I have a photo of him holding up a pair of original shackles. I've never quite been able to put into words what that image means to me. I do know that even in his young heart—he felt the spirit of our ancestors just as I did.

I was able to feel my ancestors in a more joyous way, too. Traveling through Senegal, Sylvester decided to make an unscheduled stop in this little village. It was a cattle-herding village, so it was temporary. Well, I left everything on the bus and got off to follow my guide. Suddenly, I was swarmed by a group of twelve or so young men, all calling out and trying to talk to me. I couldn't get away, and suddenly the rest of my group was pretty far ahead of me.

These young boys kept trying to get in front of the other tourists' cameras with me, but I kept resisting. When I finally caught up with Sylvester, he was talking with the tribal chief. Sylvester simply said he would help me get back to the bus to get my camera. I kept asking him what the young men were saying and he simply told me, "It's okay, just go with it." After we posed for many pictures and were on our way, he finally explained it all to me. "Those boys look at you and say you are Fulani. You are their long lost sister come back to them and they want a picture with you. They celebrate," he said. I didn't know what to say, but it touched me deeply. Looking at them as we pulled away, I recognized something distinctly familiar between us: the hard lines of the features, the brow line, the tone of the brown skin. I hadn't known. I still didn't know anything for certain, but I knew that there was a similar spirit. We all recognized it.

Another thing I remember about that trip is getting off the tour bus with twenty-two others. We stopped at this amazing tree called a Baobab and encircled it with our arms outstretched. Even in that massive circle, we could barely touch each other's hands. The significance of that tree is that the Africans use every part of it; nothing goes to waste. That made a big impression on me, no pun intended. Both Sylvester and Blaze agreed that it was a small tree, compared to what we would later see at the Baobab tree forest.

One of the customary things you do when visiting Africa is have traditional garbs made. Well, we had met this guy at the open market. When he met us later at the hotel, I told him that I wanted to see the ready-made things he had. No, he said, he custom made everything... and he wanted my money up front with a promise that he would return with my garments. For a woman born and raised on the west side of Chicago, that was a hard pill to swallow! When I refused to give him my money, he got very offended.

Blaze intervened, explaining that the man's word was his bond. "If he says he'll do it, then he'll do it." The catch was that we were getting ready to continue our travels and would be leaving town soon to head to Saly. The man promised to bring me my garments wherever we were. That just didn't sound right to me! Ultimately, I put my faith in Blaze's word just as much as in the other man's.

Much to my amazement, two days later, just as we were getting ready to leave Saly, this man showed up with my garments. He pulled up in this dinky, raggedy car with each and every piece that we had ordered. I was terribly apologetic. I tried to explain to him that, where I come from, people just don't do business that way. He wanted a little gift from me, something in return for his kindness and his word. The only nice thing I had was this satiny sort of lingerie thing. I gave that to him. Come to find out, women in Senegal treasure such things, things that we can buy at Wal-Mart.

One of the things that I had experienced while Blaze was wrapping and unwrapping his head with my scarf was the overwhelming sense that I absolutely had to come back to Africa. Ten days was not enough. I wanted to spend a year or two or three there. I came home and immediately started investigating the avenues that would let me live and work in Africa. The Mennonite church was a clear possibility, as they had been in Africa for over a hundred years. I immediately put in for a job with the MCC, the Mennonite Central Committee. Well, in early '95, they let me know about a position in the Sudan where I would be establishing the computer science department at the University of Khartoum. Despite the civil war that was going on, I was excited. The MCC had found my son an international school, and we were basically all set to proceed. And then the lottery happened. I immediately stepped in to the leadership role and couldn't abandon my family at that time. So we stayed in the States. Shortly thereafter, in late summer 1995, all Americans were ordered out of Sudan; the war had intensified.

I've made a point, though, of visiting on several other occasions. The second time, in 1996, it was a group of about sixteen of us, includ-

ing Khalif, my brother, his wife, my sister-in-law, our minister, and a group from the church. We went to Ghana. The group stayed for ten days or so, but I went back to Senegal after they left. I had already decided that if I ever went back to Africa, I was staying for a month, no two ways about it. Blaze and I had exchanged numbers the first time. He had told me that he would be there for me when I came back. I found him the second time and hired him as my tour guide. Africans are people of their word, and Blaze was no exception.

In 1997, I went back yet again. I wanted to get my hair braided. In Chicago, the little micro-braids would cost me four or five hundred dollars and take a day or more to complete. It occurred to me that for not much more, maybe six hundred dollars, I could get a plane ticket and go back to the salon in Ghana. On the Ghana trip, I had been in a time crunch, but my female tour guide, Rosemund, swore to me that this woman could have my hair braided in two hours flat. So I went with it. I gave her the equivalent of about twenty dollars along with a twenty-dollar tip. Before I knew it, I was surrounded by six or eight women who came in and started working on different sections of my hair. Sure enough, two hours later, I was on my way. I stayed for a week that time in 1997 and came home with some phenomenal micro braids and some great African fabrics.

Maybe I'll have the chance to go back again one day. There are still so many things I want to experience. Even more, I just want to feel that unspoken sense of familiarity again. I want to feel like I know things about myself that no one has ever told me... or ever needs to.

RATS AND APPLES

By the early 90s, I had seen enough signs and omens in my life that I was fully aware of them. 1992 was a big year for my family. We lost my sister, I left Xerox, and I moved back to Chicago. Early '93 found me busying myself with making Mama's basement into a nice living space for Khalif and me. It served three purposes: I would create a living space, and learn how to do the things my mom had done while building the family home, such as building walls and laying floors. I'd also be able to provide her a finished basement, something she had said she wanted over the years.

At the time, we were all feeling a little raw and just trying to stay focused on moving ahead in a positive direction. Having been through so much change, I was especially open to signs and signals and what they were telling me.

One afternoon in early spring, Mama and I decided to mow the lawn. Winter had come and gone, and the yard was more than ready for a good spring-cleaning; the grass had grown pretty tall. Now, Mama had a bad back, so naturally I was doing most of the work. I got started, mowed a little patch, and had to stop to avoid plowing right over a dead rat! I mowed a little more and had to stop again. Over and over again I found dead rats… all over the yard!

Of course, every big city has a rat problem. Chicago is notoriously bad about it! The weird thing is that my dad had taken steps to prevent that problem. Our house was built a little higher than most. The yard, the whole property, is elevated from the back of the alley by about eighteen inches. Also, he had put two 2x10 boards as a footing around the back and sides of the property, to hold the extra dirt that provided the elevation off of the alley, blocking the rats from getting in. Well, nearly thirty years had passed, and I did notice that morning that the rats had chewed holes through the now rotting old boards. It was strange, though, that we had *never* had a rat problem before that.

After having had dreams about rats, I didn't like the feeling I had that morning picking up dead ones all around the yard. It made sense to me, though. I had left an organization that was toxic to my well-being. My sister had passed away. My family had been through a tough time. I could only hope that the fact that the rats I found were dead—and not running all over the place—meant that the hard times were about to change, that better things were coming.

When the next spring came, I was fully prepared to face my task. We certainly hadn't had the money to fix up the yard and replace the gnawed boards. I bought big gloves and carried a shovel this time, fully anticipating another round of rat removal. I mowed slowly, constantly scanning for furry bodies. I couldn't believe it… With every strip of lawn, my expectations were blown. I made it completely through the job without finding a single rat! *We must be doing something right!* I thought.

That fall, a glorious evidence of that bounty appeared in a tangible form. Twenty years or so before, Mama had bought two apples trees and planted them in the backyard. They had to be planted in pairs in order to fully cross-pollinate. Well, one of them had been damaged years before and Mama had torn it out, leaving the other tree to fend for itself and barely produce. It went on to produce—on a good year—maybe half a bushel of apples, and Mama was thrilled just to get that much. In fact, she usually got so few apples that she would go on our church's annual apple-picking trip to the apple orchards to get two bushels so that she could make and can her awesome apple butter.

By the time the apples were ready for picking that year, Mama had been in bed with a bad back for a while. Giving Khalif and me the small bushel basket, she asked us to go out and pick the apples for her. We did, not thinking much of it. Well, in no time, that little basket was full, and I sent my son in to ask his grandma for another basket. She was pleased with the news and sent him to the basement to get a second one. When we filled that one, he went back again. This time, he said that Mama had sat up in bed with surprise and told him to empty an old basket that was full of tools. When he went in a third time, Mama got out of bed and followed him in disbelief. By that time, my brother and his wife were there, too, helping us pick. In sheer amazement, Mama was in the dining room looking over all these apples—three and a half bushels full!

Never had that tree given such a bounty, nor has it ever since. As a very religious and spiritual woman, Mama was quick to point out the symbolism in the abundance. It was God's way of saying that we were pleasing in his sight and that good things were to come for us. If we had only known what lay in store for us!

5

Numbers and Dreams

I have had a lot of symbolic dreams in my life but nothing like the one I had in the spring of 1995. I've always dreamt in color, bright vivid color. The images have always been metaphoric and somewhat cryptic. Not so with this dream!

The image that woke me from a sound sleep was a black and white newspaper headline, as if it was rolling fresh off the press. It was like something out of an old movie. When the image stopped it said plain as day, "JUNE 19TH" in big, bold, black, block letters and numbers. I sat bolt upright in bed with no idea what that date meant.

I speculated for a bit on what that date could possibly mean. The only thing I could come up with was Juneteenth, but that doesn't fall on the 19th. Maybe, I thought, the blues musician I had been dating would be back in town then. As usual, though, I consulted my dream interpreter. Mama, that is. She told me something I had never known. June 19th was my parents' wedding anniversary. Married in 1950, that year would have been their 45th anniversary. Funny, I had never even thought about their anniversary; it just wasn't something that I ever remember being celebrated.

Well, June 19th came and went and I was on the lookout for something else special to happen just in case the dream alluded to something more than my parents' anniversary. The day passed and not a thing worth mentioning had happened except that my brother had come in from work and wrenched his back picking up Mama's little Pekinese dog of all things. I took him to the doctor later that morning, and his doctor prescribed muscle relaxants and told him to stay home from work and rest his back.

A couple of days later, on a Wednesday, my mother and I were downstairs watching all of the excitement on the news. My brother was upstairs, knocked out with his meds. The Illinois Lottery was at a record high of $45 million. Apparently, there had been only one winning ticket sold, and officials were waiting for someone to come forward. By the next day, still no one had claimed the prize. It was June 22nd, my father's birthday. The news coverage mentioned that the ticket had been purchased at a White Hen Pantry right here in the city. It was likely that the winner was a Chicago resident.

Well, all of a sudden, we heard the biggest, most horrible noise. It was my brother stumbling down the stairs, all red-faced, leaning against the wall. He looked like he was in shock, and we thought he'd fallen. He was stuttering and stammering, trying to talk, and we were asking if he was okay, talking over each other. Finally, he said very clearly, "How does $45 million sound?"

My brother explained later that, in the haze of muscle relaxants, the news coverage finally got his attention when the report said the ticket had been bought at the White Hen Pantry, his usual spot. Normally, he wouldn't have stopped or bought the ticket that day. He would normally have bought it the night before because he and his buddies from work went there during their break. But when they went, the machines were down, so he couldn't cash in his fifty-dollar scratcher ticket. As he tells it, he had been on his way home the next morning when something told him to stop to see if the machines were working yet. They were, and he bought his five–dollar Quick Pick and headed home.

The entire city of Chicago was on alert for two days for the sole winner of the record jackpot while my brother was resting in a prescription drug induced haze. It took us many months to recognize the significance of the dream and the dates. On some level, though, I guess we all knew what was going on before it ever happened. I don't pretend to understand how all of those numbers—the 19th... the $45 million and the 45th wedding anniversary... the 22nd, my Dad's birthday—came together to change life so drastically for my family. I'm just glad that they did!

THE LOTTERY

The words my brother had said kept ringing in my head. "How does $45 million sound?" He had to wait until his wife got home from school. Once we had the whole family together that evening, we all huddled around Mama's kitchen table. No one could sleep. We couldn't even begin to wrap our heads around what our next step should be, much less about how that much money would change our lives forever. We closed all the windows and locked all the doors. I didn't expect to be scared, but I was. Everything felt new in a very strange way.

The first thing we did was pray. We asked God to protect our family and guide us through everything that was going to happen, all of us knowing that change was coming in some really big ways. My mind was working overtime. I knew that we needed some kind of structure. I told everyone that we would need to hire an attorney and also said that while each of us had always intended to take care of one another, especially of Mama, this kind of money was going to change everything and that we needed to start thinking like a corporation. No one was anywhere near ready to think that far yet. My own head was spinning, too. By that time, I was pretty close to the end of the income I was getting after leaving Xerox. We were all teetering on the line of being totally broke. In fact, we were so broke that I used to joke, "We were so broke that even the turtle was on dog food!" (Luckily, he loved it!)

By the time morning came, no one had slept a wink. Finally, my sister-in-law said something to the effect of, "I won't believe it until I see it."

So we all said, "Just call them! Call the office! Isn't there a number on the back of the ticket?"

I made the first phone call to figure out what we were supposed to do, who we were supposed to call. We all assured ourselves that they didn't have some cryptic way of tracing our call or seeing our number show up on some display. My brother made the next call, I think.

"What do we do if we really have all six numbers?" he asked.

"If you do, you need to go the Lottery Office."

A bunch of us—my brother, his wife, her sister, my older sister, her boyfriend, and I— piled into their van, got some coffee, and headed out to meet our fate. Well, it was a great plan, but the woman had sent us to the wrong office! Come to find out, that office was for people who had won less than six hundred dollars. We had been directed to the State Building. We all piled out, with my brother holding the ticket tightly. Together we went through the lobby with its gorgeous atrium in the center, walking in a haze of excitement, fear, and sleep deprivation. We just wanted to hear something definitive. Up the escalator, down the hall to the lottery office, and there on the door was the sign: "We'll be back… at 2:15." We just stood there dumbfounded and paranoid for a minute; we all had a nervous chuckle at that one. "Okay," I said. "Let's just try to act normal. We'll go down to the lobby and get some more coffee while we wait. It'll be fine." We did and twenty minutes or so later, we went back up.

My brother strode in ahead of all of us and announced, "Well, I think I have a winning ticket."

The lady behind the desk, after looking at the ticket, came out all excited. "Oh my God!" She and the other employees gathered around. It all became a blur to me. We were scared to death, trying to be so discreet, and these hysterical women that we didn't know or trust were running around yelling, "They have the ticket! These are them! It's the winners!" I literally had tears in my eyes.

"You have to go down to the other office on St. Claire Street," the main woman told us.

By that point, there were all kinds of strangers coming in and taking pictures, or asking to, with my brother. The only thing I could think was, *How the heck are we supposed to get safely down to St. Claire Street now that you've announced to the entire city that we're basically in possession of $45 million!?* I imagined someone coming up to us with a gun, making us choose between the ticket and our lives!

Well, somebody had to escort us out of the building; it was a state policewoman, and a small throng of people followed us. Once we were in the taxicab, though, we were on our own. The ride went fine, but, of course, the press had already been notified and was waiting for us when we got there—just that fast! But that's why we had come in numbers: safety. I, for one, didn't want my picture taken. I wanted to stay under the radar. My brother and sister-in-law didn't mind at all, though.

Anyway, in the office, Desiree, who was the head of the Lottery Agency at that time, told us exactly what I had been telling my family. "You need to get an attorney." She was so emphatic about it that she even told us we didn't have to turn in the ticket at that time. Her advice was to get an attorney beforehand to figure out some of the legalities. "Figure out how you're going to collect these funds, for one thing," she told us. It was good for my family to hear it from someone other than me. She referred us to a few good law firms. "You can secure your ticket. It's yours and that's not going to change. Just take your time and do it right."

That's exactly what we did. We took our time. We talked to several law firms and several banks. We thought that the one bank we were referred to was going to be perfect. It was very well established, and there were several women on the team with whom we met. Everything was going well, and then the man who was doing most of the speaking started espousing the fact that the bank was associated with "old money." He was so proud of that fact and really thought that he impressed us with it. The problem was, "old money" to most black folks is a contradiction of terms. Most of us didn't have money back in the day, don't have family money to live on generation after generation, and don't have much of it now. We certainly didn't. So it didn't make sense to us. I mean, when I think of old money, I think of the Rockefellers. It almost seemed as if he was trying to tell us that we would suddenly become something we are not. We had no interest in "becoming" anything.

Another thing that rubbed me wrong personally was that he kept correcting or amending things that the women on his team would say.

It was just rude. We had a system of review in place with our attorneys, which allowed me to *indirectly* call him out on it. I told our attorney that it appeared as if this guy was the slave master dictating to his three wives. In my mind, he would have been better off if he'd just let them speak for him! Another check against them was, unfortunately, that they didn't include Daryl in the team that met with us. Daryl was named one of the top VPs in banking, and he was a black man, one we wanted to meet. Come to find out, our attorney informed us that the bank was so shocked about not getting the account that, as a result of meeting with us, its employees were going to go through "diversity training" in order to understand and learn how to interact with people of different cultures. Talk about amazing!

The other bank team we met with essentially offered the same things and used the same industry language, save the "old money" line. It was a completely different feeling, though. We decided to do business with them. Our main attorney was named Demetrius, and he took the crazy ride through it all with us. I remember laughing to myself; these men were so serious, and my brother remarked how much this team of lawyers looked like a bunch of Dick Tracy movie characters in their broad shouldered suits.

An interesting thing happened in the course of our initial meetings. I guess partly because I had worked in a professional, corporate environment, every time our attorney or the bankers posed a question, my brother would pause and look at his wife, and then they would both look at me. Then I would answer. I think that he probably was a little (or maybe a lot) intimidated, and certainly was in shock, as we all were by the magnitude of this. No one had ever really addressed him as "Mr. Britton" before, at least not like this, and I think it kind of freaked him out a bit. He had been a steelworker for years and knew nothing of this new environment. By default, I sort of became the family advisor and liaison between us and the bankers and lawyers. The role came naturally for me. It felt like a repeat of so many situations and relationships I had had ever since leaving home during high school. This time, though, I got to help my family. I didn't always feel like the wise one, however. Most of this was new to me, too, so I got to be the one asking the stupid questions.

One of the things I insisted on was that, aside from an initial financial advance to get us through the first two months or so, we forego our regular payments until all of the business matters were firmly in place and we all got educated on the ABCs of handling our money for the long-term—finances and money management 101. The bank respected our wishes and set up a six or eight week course for us that was taught by their personnel. Believe me, this was no ordinary class or conference room! I didn't know there was such a place in any bank. It was the main banking headquarters in downtown Chicago, and every week we got to sit at what seemed like a twenty-foot long solid oak table in a wood-paneled room with elaborate paintings and stained windows that looked like they'd been taken from a castle in England or something. We intentionally tried to create some levity, just to try to feel comfortable, by imagining things like the panels covering secret passageways. And maybe they did! The bankers constantly bestowed food and gifts, like fancy stationary and pens, on us, too.

The banking team was very kind to us, even respecting our wish that every class and every meeting be opened with a prayer. Several weeks into this relationship, we didn't have to make the request. They automatically initiated the prayers themselves. We ended up meeting at least once a week for quite a while. After that, each of us had individual meetings to structure what we needed for ourselves. We all learned about investing and planning for long term income.

As a result of all of our research and planning with our legal team, we established ourselves as an LLC. There were a lot of legal considerations aside from just the money itself. My sister-in-law, who loved teaching, had to come to terms with the fact that she would have to give up her career. There are just so many inherent liabilities with having large sums of money. You can be sued, even if the claims are fabricated. She and my brother had to get an umbrella insurance policy to make sure that they were all safe and secure.

All in all, we were getting a lot of exposure. After all, my brother had won the largest lottery ever taken by a single ticket in the city of

Chicago. My brother and sister did the Oprah show, in fact, some-time during that first six-month period, and again later on. We were all there for that first one, including Demetrius, our lawyer, and Lyle, our banker. I think my favorite part of that experience, though was not all of the media stuff. It was Mr. D (Demetrius) nudging me on the back and saying quietly to me, "They had Annette" every time Oprah asked my brother or his wife a question. "Well, weren't you scared? How did you do this? How did you do that?" Demetrius just kept on with, "They had Annette!" It was funny. I became sort of the bulldog, like "They've got Annette and nobody's gonna mess with them!"

So we got off on a good foot. Despite our best efforts at staying grounded and levelheaded, though, a case of LFF set in... and it was highly contagious. LFF stood for what I called the Lotto Fever Factor. The duration of this state is about five years. It's sort of the mingling of excitement, fear, speculation, intimidation, audacity, and an over-whelming sense of blessing mixed with a giant dose of *just plain crazy* that comes with the almighty dollar in such large amounts.

LFF was pervasive; it hit everyone we knew and many more people that we didn't know. Cousins, whom we knew but had never visited, started showing up in the black of night or during pouring rainstorms. I remember looking out the window and seeing this figure all in black with a trench coat in the pouring rain one time. Scared the daylights out of all of us! Even when people don't ask for anything, you know why they've appeared out of the clear blue: LFF!

My brother even started something called the Lotto Box. It was this box that he would keep all of the letters we got from total strangers asking us for money. "I need $68,000 to fix my house... I need X-amount for my mother's surgery... I need, I need, I need..." He still has that box somewhere. It's just amazing how quickly people learn about what you have and how audaciously they decide that they are entitled to it.

Now, my grandfather was ninety two years old at the time. I would say if anyone had a reason to be impatient for the money, it was him. He felt he was living on borrowed time and wanted to do some

115

living with that money while he could. I'll never forget it. One day he just started throwing furniture around and hauling stuff out into the yard to get rid of it. He called my brother and asked him to come and get all of that stuff so he could buy new furniture. I remember sitting with him in the front yard and him asking me, with this pleading look on his tired face, "Why is it taking so long?" He had no interest in anything I had to say about taking the time to learn to handle money. He just knew his grandson was a "millionaire," and he wanted to enjoy it while he had the chance.

Even the professionals got hit with LFF. Our team would start talking sometimes, and I felt like I had to rein them in. The excitement just overtook people and they would start talking like little kids on the brink of a great adventure or something. And there I was saying, "Hold up a second—you're supposed to be the attorney!" But, again, we had won one of, if not the biggest single jackpot in the history of Chicago winners of the Illinois lottery at the time. It *was* a big deal.

It even hit us for a bit, even levelheaded me. In '95, after the bank was telling us what kind of clout and buying power we had, I told my brother that he should go buy a Hummer. He said, "Nah, I don't want one of those." I told him at least we could go test drive one. The banker agreed, saying we could ask to test drive probably anything we wanted, and that they would even let us keep something for a few days. I told my brother that, even if he didn't want to go for it, I did. Ultimately, we never did buy anything that extravagant, but it was a nice fantasy! We didn't event do the test drive!

We did all end up with new cars (nothing fancy) and new homes. My brother and his wife bought spacious, gorgeous condos for themselves and for my mom and grandparents in downtown Chicago. They wanted to buy me a house, too, but I knew from the beginning that it just wouldn't be possible for several reasons. First of all, the accountant explained to them the sticky situation with the federal laws regarding gift giving and allowable amounts. The other option was to create a trust, but I wanted something that was actually *mine*, not something that ultimately belonged to my brother. I told him and his wife that I appreciated the gesture but really needed to take care of my son and me by myself. I was prepared to buy my own house. It felt like such a breath of fresh air when I started looking around and realized that I could afford my own condo, too. It might not have been up to my brother's standards, but it would be mine, and that was the important thing. It was a small, two-bedroom place, and it suited Khalif and me to a T!

As for Mom, my brother and my sister-in-law, they have wonderful condos, approximately three or four thousand square feet each. Both condos were two smaller units combined into one, so they have more than ample space. Now that I'm in Phoenix, I love going back to Chicago and visiting my mama. She has the most beautiful view from her place. Through a very large wall of windows that overlook the lake to the east and the harbor to the south, you can see all of downtown Chicago. My brother loves to look out his windows with his high-powered binoculars, telescope, and cameras. He's got some phenomenal pictures, truly one-of-a-kind shots, of Chicago. They've built a good life there.

The lottery changed our lives that year. Looking back, I'm really proud of the way that my family has evolved in this amazing process. My stepping into the advisor role really was just sort of a natural progression, and I'm so happy to have been able to offer that sort of foundation for them, or at least to be a part of guiding them toward creating that foundation. Together, we addressed one by one all of the fears I had in those first few weeks as we huddled and brainstormed around Mama's kitchen table.

I think that I heard the expression of those fears most clearly during one of the Oprah show tapings. She had on a number of guests who had won lotteries. One woman was saying that she had won ten million dollars or something and had completely fallen out with her family over their resentments. While she had helped them and given them something, it was just never enough for any of them. The money became the bottom line. One of her sisters actually admitted to Oprah, "It's not that I have *a right* to her money. I just have a *want* to more of her money." It was fascinating and kind of frightening all at once.

Before we ever did the Oprah show, I actually asked our banker to give me some statistics, some numbers, and some cold hard facts about how most lottery winners fare after they get the money. It was pretty dismal! The fact is that most people overspend and eventually lose most of their money paying back the debt they've gotten into.

Another woman on the Oprah show told the story of how she over-spent almost immediately. Even though she was a "millionaire," she was so in debt and had so many people coming after her that she had to get a job. The problem was that no one in her community would hire her. She had to leave the state and ended up working the night shift at a 7/11 or something. It seemed so unreal to me, and so avoidable.

Then there was this other man, an older man. He said that one of his family members actually put a contract out on his life for not sharing—in their opinion—enough of his money with them. So sad!

The bottom line is that when you're just working a normal sort of job and a low-profile life, you know that if you've only got fifty bucks till payday, you budget it. When you walk down the street, people don't recognize you and harass you, looking for a handout. When you suddenly have millions, though, everyone—including well-meaning charities and yourself—thinks there's a huge surplus. If you're not careful, it's way too easy to default to thinking that the interest your money is making will increase exponentially and offset any debt you incur.

That is exactly what I wanted my family to understand. I think that, working together, we did a pretty good job of educating ourselves along those lines. I can honestly say, looking back, that I knew full well when I left Xerox that I was taking a huge leap of faith. I just knew that it was time to go. I remember telling myself, *I'm being prepared for something.* I didn't know what that something was, but I've always been good at following that feeling in my gut and knowing that I will be led to discover whatever the source and goal of that feeling might be. What it comes down to for me is faith in my most high God. I knew that it was He who was preparing me and He who would show me the way. The truth in that feeling extended to my family. When we won the lottery, I didn't want us to be just another casualty of avarice. I wanted us to be a success, to use the gift we had been entrusted with to the best of our abilities.

It was fear that drove me, really. I was motivated by my fear once we actually knew that the money was ours. But if that fear was God-given—and I know that it was—then I am grateful for it. It was instrumental in putting us on course and keeping us there. As we move toward the last years of our annual lottery checks, I know that the lessons learned from those initial fears will help us to build an even stronger foundation, a business that will sustain us and bring a greater good to the world. And that is exactly what we are ALL being prepared for. The lottery and all of the aftermath is really just part of the bigger plan.

5

ANOTHER SIGN— ANOTHER BOUNTY

I've said it before, but my life has been one full of signs and symbols. I guess most people's lives are that way. Some of us have been given the gift of being attuned to those signs and symbols. I'd like to think, with the help of Mama's dream-interpretations, I've done a pretty good job of understanding what they mean.

In the spring of 2005, nearly a full decade after we had been blessed with the lottery winnings, the sign of another bounty came our way. Of course, the apple tree had produced an un-foretold wealth of fruit the fall before that fateful June 19 of 1995. Well, ten years later, we harvested another fruit. Our little dwarf pear tree at Mama's house, which had just sort of subsisted for half as long as the apple tree, suddenly experienced a surge of abundance. We picked bushel after bushel of some of the largest, most beautiful pears we had ever seen. With several people helping, it was impossible to keep track of how many we picked and gave away, but everyone agreed that those pears put to shame anything you'd find in the grocery store; the word "dwarf" didn't do them justice.

Mama recognized what was going on immediately. "It's another fruit. Another kind of bounty is coming our way," she said with that familiar little glint in her eyes. I was thinking the same thing and started saying prayers to God that he would prepare me—and the rest of us—for whatever it was and that we would recognize it when it came our way.

Well, I had heard of this thing called The Dreaming Room, the brainchild of entrepreneurial guru Mr. Michael Gerber, at the 1st Annual Entrepreneur Conference in Phoenix in November of 2006. Ever so gently, I could feel a stirring again. However vaguely I sensed it, I knew that I needed to go to the Dreaming Room event.

As fate would have it, the holidays were upon us, and there was this deep sense that we all needed to be together, so that became the focus—a family Christmas. Then my sister, just two years older than me, took ill quite suddenly. I went to be with her, which pushed The Dreaming Room and Michael Gerber far from my mind.

As summer of 2007 approached, I found myself caring for my now terminally ill sister. She had been given a diagnosis: late stage, small cell lung cancer. She had six months to live, maybe a year. I was exhausted as I came home in late May for a break. My sweetheart, Henry, had become insistent on my attending this upcoming Dreaming Room event in San Diego. It was as though he knew that this was to be the place for my lifelong purpose to manifest itself. But I had just returned home after being gone since February, and I refused! Henry persisted. "You've got to do this for you," he said. "For that book that is inside you." Very, very, extremely reluctantly I finally agreed to go.

On June 22, 2007 (again, my father's birthday) I met two men who would have a huge impact on my life. First of all, of course, I met Mr. Gerber. As I sat there in the hot seat, I watched some of the stories in this collection flow out of me like I was a wide open faucet. These stories had been bottled up inside. The dream of writing them was my reason for being in Phoenix for the past six years. I watched and listened as they flowed, and I also spilled my passion for the concept of FBW. With tears streaming down my face, I knew that I was on to something.

In that room was also the man who would help me to find a voice for my stories and a foundation for FBW. Corey Blake and I talked many times over those three days. Along with Mr. Gerber, he encouraged me to get my stories down on paper... and then out into the world as the inspiration for my business concept. While I had always seen the interconnectedness of my life's experiences, that day I began to see more fully the momentum with which all of them had led me to this point... and beyond.

I began working with Corey and Eva Silva Travers. In a series of twenty or so phone calls, I relayed the stories of my life to them. Slowly but surely, I began to feel little butterfly sensations all through me. Things were moving, stirring, and breaking free. They had to breathe and move before they could fly out of me and move through the world in the way they were intended. It's their purpose. And as they fly, they carry with them the roots and the foundation—and the future—of Five Black Women… Inc.

Son, I have put the baby down.

About the Author

Annette Y. Britton is an entrepreneur, businesswoman, mother and founder of Five Black Women, Inc. Born in Chicago's inner city, during her teen years Annette lived on a Mennonite farm while attending high school. Out of college, she worked for Xerox Corp for 9 years as an electronic engineer before venturing out on her own. Her experience of life from the perspectives of great poverty and great wealth have fueled her passion to transform the world, one community, one person at a time. Her most recent endeavor is as a storyteller and author. Currently, Annette commutes between Phoenix and Chicago and calls both home.

LaVergne, TN USA
30 September 2010
199080LV00004B/2/P

9 780982 220665